Safe Sanctuaries

Reducing the Risk of Child Abuse in the Church

by Joy T. Melton

DISCIPLESHIP RESOURCES

P.O. BOX 840 • NASHVILLE, TENNESSEE 37202-0840
http://www.discipleshipresources.org

Dedication

This book is dedicated, with gratitude, to the members of First United Methodist Church in Cherryville, North Carolina, and especially to those who have worked in the church's nursery, loving each and every child who has been entrusted to their care. A particular word of thanks must be said for the ministry of Mrs. Lola Beam and Mrs. Dell Wofford, both of whom have been providing a safe and love-filled church home to the children of First UMC since I was a child. They have modeled, for nearly four decades, my congregation's commitment to caring for children, and there are many others, in addition to my two sisters and me, who have been blessed by their love.

This book is also dedicated to John and Teddy Kilby, W.T. and Teenie Robinson, and Buddy and Jane Robinson, for the unfailing love with which they surrounded me and gave me a sacred sanctuary in which to safely grow in the way that leads to a life of enduring faith.

Finally, this book is dedicated to David and Kathryn Melton, in the hope that we will always be together on the journey of faith.

Scripture quotations, unless otherwise indicated, are from the New Revised Standard Version of the Bible, copyright ©1989 by the Division of Christian Education of the National Council of Churches of Christ in the United States of America.

Library of Congress Card Catalog No. 97-66519

ISBN 0-88177-220-8

This resource is published by Discipleship Resources in the hope that it will help congregations in planning. Discipleship Resources and the General Board of Discipleship are not engaged in legal, accounting, or other professional advising services. If legal advice or other expert assistance is required, the services of a professional advisor should be sought. This book does not establish a standard of care for local churches. Each local church makes its own decisions and determines what is best for it, and this book is intended only to provide information that may be helpful to some churches.

DR220

Table of Contents

CHAPTER ONE
Our Mandate.. 5

CHAPTER TWO
The Scope of the Problem 11

CHAPTER THREE
Recruiting, Screening, and Hiring Workers 23

CHAPTER FOUR
Basic Procedures for Safe Ministry with Children and Youth............. 31

CHAPTER FIVE
Developing a Congregational Plan for Responding to Allegations of Abuse 37

CHAPTER SIX
Implementation Strategies for the Congregation............................ 43

CHAPTER SEVEN
A Model for Training Workers 51

CHAPTER EIGHT
After Abuse, Then What? 55

CHAPTER NINE
Sample Forms 61

CHAPTER TEN
Other Sources and Resources.. 79

Our Mandate

AS CHRISTIANS, we are called to live according to the gospel of Jesus Christ. Our Christian heritage derives from that of the Hebrews. We accept the tradition and experience set forth in the Old Testament Scriptures as our own. In the history of the ancient Hebrews, we find a deeply rooted legacy of justice and mercy. (See Micah 6:8, Isaiah 1:17, Amos 5:24, Isaiah 56:1, Deuteronomy 24:17, Leviticus 19:15.) We also find a strong tradition of hospitality and generosity. (See Isaiah 58:10-12 and Leviticus 19:10.)

Justice and hospitality were essential elements of the covenant between the people and God. Worship was the lifeblood of the covenant. Throughout the history of the Hebrew people, their practice of worshiping God in holy places is recorded. At times, the holy place was no more than a small tent or a pile of rocks made on the plains. At other times, the holy place was a beautifully ornate temple with many grand chambers. No matter what the place of worship looked like, the people treasured it as a holy place, a sanctuary, where they were able to worship in safety and harmony. (See Psalms 20:1-2 and Psalms 27:4-5.) Today, we must remember that our churches are holy places of sanctuary for the children of God. Our churches must continue to be places where people of all ages can come together for worship, study, and service, with the assurance that they are safe and secure in the community of faith.

The New Testament makes clear that as Christians we continue in a covenant relationship with God and with the whole community of faith. We must live just and generous lives, following the great commandments set forth by Jesus Christ. Jesus plainly taught that children were to be included and provided for within the community of faith. (See Luke 18:15-17 and Matthew 18:5-6.) Throughout the history of the Christian church, children have been included in the worship and ministry of the community of faith. Today, the church may be the only place where some children find the unconditional love and care they so desperately need to grow, to thrive, and to become faithful people. As Christians, we must take our responsibilities to our chil-

Notes:
_____

_____
_____
_____
_____
_____
_____
_____
_____
_____
_____
_____
_____
_____
_____

BUT JESUS CALLED FOR THEM
and said, "Let the little children come to me, and do not stop them; for it is to such as these that the kingdom of God belongs."

Luke 18:16

dren very seriously, always attending to their spiritual growth and nurturing. We fail in our responsibilities if we neglect to take adequate precautions against physical abuse in our churches. It is unlikely that we can completely prevent child abuse in every circumstance. Yet, it is possible for us to greatly reduce the risk by following a thorough and practical policy of prevention.

Child sexual abuse is a tragic reality in our communities. Although we would much prefer to deny the reality, child sexual abuse in our churches is an inescapable fact. All too often we hear reports in the media about abuse perpetrated in a church or a church-sponsored program. When I began work in the ministry nearly two decades ago, there was little public awareness of the existence of child sexual abuse in the church. Now, as an attorney and a United Methodist minister, I know that it is the single most traumatic issue I deal with in my work.

United Methodist churches have historically worked to assure that children in the communities were cared for with food, clothing, education, and an affirmation of value and self-worth. In many communities, The United Methodist Church (through its predecessor denominations) was the first to provide kindergarten for the children of the community, daycare centers for children of working parents, and Sunday schools where the children heard about God's love and presence in daily life. Today, these traditions continue and provide a solid foundation from which we can address the need for prevention of all forms of child abuse.

When allegations of child abuse in the church are made, whether they eventually are proven true or false, everyone in the church suffers. The child victim and his or her family suffer encompassing pain. The congregation suffers the trauma of knowing that its life-giving covenant has been broken. The family of the perpetrator suffers intense humiliation and a likely break-up of the family unit. Often when such allegations are made, litigation is the result. Criminal charges may be brought against the suspected perpetrator, or a civil lawsuit may be filed to recover monetary damages from the accused and from the local church. The costs of litigation, regardless of the outcome, are astronomical—financially, emotionally, and spiritually. These losses are experienced by all who are involved. In many such situations, it takes years to feel that the wholeness of the community of faith has been restored.

Even when allegations of child sexual abuse are proved false, the grief and trauma experienced within the church take an enormous toll. The person who is falsely accused and his or her family are terribly wronged and humiliated. The congregation is guilt-ridden about how abuse could happen in their midst; then the congregation suffers with the accused when the allegations are proved false. Finally, we must recognize that the victim who made false allegations is in need of the love and nurture of the faith community.

The 1996 General Conference of The United Methodist Church adopted a resolution aimed at reducing the risk of child sexual abuse in the church. The full text of this resolution is printed on the next two pages. As you read it you will notice that specific steps are to be taken by local churches, annual conferences, the General Board of Discipleship, and the General Board of Global Ministries. This book has been created to assist your conference or local church as you work through these steps.

Child abuse prevention and risk reduction policies and procedures are essential for every congregation, not only for the protection and safety of our children (all those under the age of eighteen) but also for our volunteer and employed workers with children. We are keenly aware that local congregations differ in the ways they engage in ministry with children and youth. Therefore, each congregation's need for prevention policies and guidelines will be somewhat different from the others.

The gospel calls us to be engaged in ministry with children and youth. We must not allow the risks to undermine or stop our ministry. Rather, we must
- acknowledge the risks and develop a practical plan to reduce them.
- take steps to prevent harm to our children and our workers.
- continue to answer the gospel's imperative to be in ministry with children, making a difference in their lives.

This resource is offered as a source of guidance and of appropriate model policies for your congregation as it creates a substantive plan of child abuse prevention. *Safe Sanctuaries* can be a valuable resource for your congregation or annual conference as it undertakes to make the gospel's mandate real by providing a safe and wholly secure place in which children may experience the abiding love of God and fellowship in the community of faith.

Notes:

WHY IMPLEMENT A PLAN TO PREVENT CHILD ABUSE?

Because our church is a community of faith—a safe haven and sanctuary—where children and youth can be confirmed and strengthened in the way that leads to life eternal.

Notes:

THE GENERAL CONFERENCE OF The United Methodist Church adopted this resolution aimed at reducing the risk of child sexual abuse in the church.

Reducing the Risk of Child Sexual Abuse in the Church

Jesus said, "Whoever welcomes [a] child...welcomes me" (Matthew 18:5). Children are our present and our future, our hope, our teachers, our inspiration. They are full participants in the life of the church and in the realm of God.

Jesus also said, "If any of you put a stumbling block before one of these little ones..., it would be better for you if a great millstone were fastened around your neck and you were drowned in the depth of the sea"(Matthew 18:6). Our Christian faith calls us to offer both hospitality and protection to the little ones, the children. The Social Principles of The United Methodist Church state that "children must be protected from economic, physical and sexual exploitation, and abuse" (¶ 66C).

Tragically, churches have not always been safe places for children. Child sexual abuse, exploitation, and ritual abuse* occur in churches, both large and small, urban and rural. The problem cuts across all economic, cultural, and racial lines. It is real, and it appears to be increasing. Most annual conferences can cite specific incidents of child sexual abuse and exploitation in their churches. Virtually every congregation has among its members adult survivors of early sexual trauma.

Such incidents are devastating to all who are involved: the child, the family, the local church and its leaders. Increasingly, churches are torn apart by the legal, emotional, and monetary consequences of litigation following allegations of abuse.

God calls us to make our churches safe places, protecting children and other vulnerable persons from sexual and ritual abuse. God calls us to create communities of faith where children and adults grow safe and strong. In response to this churchwide challenge, the following steps should be taken to reduce the risk of child sexual abuse:

A. Local churches should:
1. Develop and implement an ongoing education plan for the congregation and its leaders on the reality of child abuse, risk factors leading to child abuse, and strategies for prevention;
2. Adopt screening procedures (use of application forms, interviews, reference checks, background clearance, and so forth) for workers (paid and unpaid) directly or indirectly involved in the care of children and youth;
3. Develop and implement safety procedures for church activities such as having two or more nonrelated adults present in classroom or activity; leaving doors open and

installing half-doors or windows in doors or halls; providing hall monitors; instituting sign-in and sign-out procedures for children ages ten or younger; and so forth;

4. Advise children and young persons of an agency or a person outside as well as within the local church whom they can contact for advice and help if they have suffered abuse;

5. Carry liability insurance that includes sexual abuse coverage;

6. Assist the development of awareness and self-protection skills for children and youth through special curriculum and activities; and

7. Be familiar with annual conference and other Church policies regarding clergy sexual misconduct.

B. Annual conferences should:

1. Develop safety and risk-reducing policies and procedures for conference-sponsored events such as camps, retreats, youth gatherings, childcare at conference events, mission trips, and so forth; and

2. Develop guidelines and training processes for use by Church leaders who carry responsibility for prevention of child abuse in local churches. Both sets of policies shall be developed by a task force appointed by the cabinet in cooperation with appropriate conference agencies. These policies shall be approved by the annual conference and assigned to a conference agency for implementation. It is suggested that the policies be circulated in conference publications and shared with lay professionals and clergy at district or conference seminars.

C. The General Board of Discipleship and the General Board of Global Ministries should cooperatively develop and/or identify and promote the following resources:

1. Sample policies, procedures, forms, and so forth for reducing the risk of sexual abuse and exploitation of children and youth in local churches, both in relation to their own sponsored programs and to any outreach ministries or other programs for children or youth that use church space;

2. Child abuse prevention curriculum for use in local churches;

3. Training opportunities and other educational resources on child sexual abuse and exploitation and on ritual abuse; and

4. Resources on healing for those who have experienced childhood sexual trauma.

*"Ritual abuse" refers to abusive acts committed as part of ceremonies or rites; ritual abusers are often related to cults, or pretend to be.

See Social Principles, ¶66C; "Putting Children and Their Families First"; "Sexual Abuse Within the Ministerial Relationship and Sexual Harassment Within The United Methodist Church."

Notes:

WHY IMPLEMENT A PLAN TO PREVENT CHILD ABUSE?

Because our church is a community of faith and a safe sanctuary where children and youth can learn and develop the spiritual resources they need to face suffering and evil.

The Scope
of the Problem

EACH WEEK many local churches participate in the service of holy baptism for children. In the congregation where I worship, we have three worship services each Sunday, and often we have a baptism in each service. On a recent Sunday, we had five baptisms in one service: the baptism of a pair of twin brothers and their brothers, a set of triplets. What a celebration!

For each baptism, our pastor begins the service by reading Jesus' words, "Let the little children come to me, and do not stop them; for it is to such as these that the kingdom of heaven belongs" (Matthew 19:14). The parents and the congregation are examined as to their willingness to raise the child(ren) in the way that leads to faith, the child is named and baptized, and then the child is presented to the congregation. At this point, the congregation assumes a *holy responsibility* as it replies, "With God's help we will so order our lives after the example of Christ, that *this child,* surrounded by steadfast love, may be established in the faith, and confirmed and strengthened in the way that leads to life eternal"(*The United Methodist Hymnal*, p. 44). By our pledge, we commit to lead the child, by the example of our lives, into a life of Christian faith. By our pledge, we commit to support the parents in their efforts to lead their child into a life of Christian faith. By our pledge, we vow to keep our church a holy place in which all children may come to know God and experience the love of Jesus Christ. When we think seriously about the promise we make in the baptismal service, we can only conclude that we are truly called to prevent child abuse in our churches.

Anyone who reads newspapers, watches television, or listens to the radio knows that child abuse and violence against children happen all too frequently in our society. Each day brings another tragic story. The reports range from allegations of sexual abuse to allegations of inappropriate forms of punishment. During a recent thirty-day period, I kept track of alleged incidents reported by the media, including: the sexual molestation of middle school students by a trusted teacher; the sexual abuse of a teenage boy by a drifter already on probation for the sexual molestation of a minor; the sexual

Notes:

WHOEVER WELCOMES ONE
such child in my name
welcomes me.
Matthew 18:5

molestation of a preschooler by her stepfather; the pornographic exploitation of a preschooler by her parents, who offered the child to acquaintances in exchange for cocaine; and the sexual abuse of a preschooler by a Sunday school teacher. The abuse happened not in dark, isolated alleys but in the child's home, the child's daycare center, the child's school classroom, the child's summer camp, and the child's church. The identities of the alleged abusers ranged from parents, to aunts and uncles, to family friends, to teachers, to childcare workers, to camp counselors, to Sunday school teachers, to complete strangers.

No matter where a child is harmed or by whom, as Christians we grieve for the inestimable injury done and for the losses experienced by the child and the child's family. As Christians, we are called to move beyond grieving to active efforts to eliminate the possibility of child abuse everywhere, and most especially in our churches. Our churches must be the safest and holiest of hallowed places for all children if we are to succeed in our efforts to make the gospel real in the lives of people in need.

The depth and breadth of the problem of child abuse is far greater than can be effectively addressed within this resource. For our purposes, we must limit our focus to the prevention of child abuse in the church and its ministries.

Types of Child Abuse

Generally, child abuse is categorized in five primary forms: physical abuse, emotional abuse, neglect, sexual abuse, and ritual abuse:

1. Physical Abuse

Abuse in which a person deliberately and intentionally causes bodily harm to a child. Examples may include violent battery with a weapon (knife, belt, strap, and so forth), burning, shaking, kicking, choking, fracturing bones, and any of a wide variety of non-accidental injuries to a child's body.

2. Emotional Abuse

Abuse in which a person exposes a child to spoken and/or unspoken violence or emotional cruelty. Emotional abuse sends a message to the child of worthlessness, badness, and being not only unloved but undeserving of love and care. Children exposed to emotional abuse may have experienced being locked in a closet, being deprived of any sign of parental affection, being constantly told they are bad or stupid, or being allowed or forced to abuse alcohol or drugs. Emotional abuse is often very difficult to prove and is devastating to the victim.

3. Neglect
Abuse in which a person endangers a child's health, safety, or welfare through negligence. Neglect may include withholding food, clothing, medical care, education, and even affection and affirmation of the child's self-worth. This is perhaps the most common form of abuse.

4. Sexual Abuse
Abuse in which sexual contact between a child and an adult (or another older and more powerful youth) occurs. The child is never truly capable of consenting to or resisting such contact and/or such sexual acts. Often, the child is physically and psychologically dependent upon the perpetrator of the abuse. Examples of sexual abuse may include fondling, intercourse, incest, and the exploitation of and exposure to child pornography or prostitution.

5. Ritual Abuse
Abuse in which physical, sexual, or psychological violations of a child are inflicted regularly, intentionally, and in a stylized way by a person or persons responsible for the child's welfare. The abuser may appeal to some higher authority or power to justify the abuse. The abuse may include cruel treatment of animals or repeated threats of harm to the child, other persons, and animals. Reports of ritual abuse are often extremely horrifying and may seem too grim to be true. Children making such reports must not be ignored.

It Can Happen Anywhere
When a child reports that he or she has experienced the behaviors detailed in these descriptions, serious attention should be paid to the report. While not every child's story is actually a report of abuse, the truth needs to be determined to prevent either further harm to the child or further false allegations.

Child abuse is criminal behavior and is punished severely in every state. Although each state has its own specific legal definition, generally speaking, child sexual abuse exploits

Notes:

WHAT IS ABUSE?
Child abuse may include
- Physical Abuse
- Emotional Abuse
- Neglect
- Sexual Abuse
- Ritual Abuse

Notes:

_____

_____

_____

_____

_____

_____

_____

_____

_____

_____

THE CHILD VICTIM IS NEVER
responsible for causing the abuse, and the child victim is never to be blamed for the abuse.

and harms children by involving them in sexual behavior for which they are unprepared, to which they cannot consent, and from which they are unable to protect themselves.

The child victim is **never responsible** for causing the abuse, and the child victim is **never to be blamed** for the abuse. The child victim is **never capable of consent to abusive behavior**, either legally or morally. Child sexual abuse is **always** wrong and is solely the responsibility of the abuser.

The church must and certainly can work to assure children and families that abuse of children will not be tolerated or ignored in the community of faith. The church can demonstrate its commitment to provide a safe, secure place where all children can grow in faith and wisdom by seriously addressing the need to develop and implement abuse prevention policies and strategies for every congregation.

Frequently, when congregations are first considering the task of developing a child abuse prevention policy and strategy, one or more members may respond: "Well, this is silly. Such an awful thing would never happen in our church!" Or, "I think we're blowing this issue out of proportion—just because it happens in the big city churches doesn't mean it would ever happen here." Or, "We have a hard enough time recruiting volunteers for Sunday school and keeping the nursery. If we start making each worker answer a lot of questions and sign a covenant we'll scare everybody off— then what will we do?" Or, "I don't see much point in this since we don't have any children in this church."

These comments reflect not only our reluctance to admit that the horrors of child abuse are real for a large number of children, but they also reflect our complete abhorrence of the thought that such crimes could happen in our churches—our very holiest of places! Perhaps comments like these reveal our unfailing optimism that in "our church" atrocities cannot happen.

Before their work in devising abuse prevention strategies is complete, members will inevitably learn that no church is immune from the horrors of child abuse simply because it wishes to be. During the course of their work, they may hear about an incident in the church across the street; or a member of the congregation will reveal that he or she is a survivor of childhood abuse and is grateful that the congregation is taking this task so seriously; or a child's parent will report a suspected incident of abuse to the pastor. Without a doubt, the congregation's work will take on a new and deeper sense of importance when revelations from "close to home" are made known.

Knowing the Facts

When child abuse occurs in our own neighborhoods, it gets our attention and sometimes serves as a catalyst in a way that nameless and faceless children counted in statistics cannot. However, it is important to be familiar with a few statistics:

- The National Committee to Prevent Child Abuse, based in Chicago, IL, reports that in 1997 over 3,000,000 children were reported for child abuse and neglect to child protective service agencies in the U.S.
- Studies have estimated that 1 out of 3 girls is sexually abused before the age of 18. Similarly, studies indicate 1 out of 7 boys have been sexually abused before the age of 18. Even more frightening is that these numbers may be underestimated since many children are reluctant to report abuse.
- The National Committee for the Prevention of Child Abuse in the United States of America reports that 2000 deaths attributable to child abuse and/or neglect occur each year.

Let's think again about the first number listed: three million incidents of abuse per year. That equals 8,219 children abused each day; 343 children abused per hour; nearly 6 (5.7) children abused every minute; and one child abused every 10-12 seconds of every hour of every day, including Sabbath.

The Church at Risk

In light of the statistics, it seems that any organization involved with children is a place where abuse could occur. What makes the risk for churches especially high? Several of the following factors could be named:

- Churches behave as relatively trusting organizations, relying upon their members and their leaders to conduct themselves appropriately. Sometimes this trusting attitude persists even in the face of questions or reports of misconduct.
- Churches are notoriously inactive when it comes to screening its volunteers and/or employees who work with children and youth. Often, no investigation is done

Notes:

THREE MILLION INCIDENTS OF child abuse are reported each year. That equates to one incident every 10-12 seconds around the clock, seven days a week!

Notes:

_____

_____

_____

_____

_____

_____

_____

_____

_____

_____

_____

WHILE A CHURCH CANNOT
guarantee the safety of every person, every church can be responsible for reducing and eliminating circumstances that could lead to harm or injury.

at all before total strangers are welcomed aboard.

- Churches routinely provide opportunities for close contact and for close personal relationships with children. Indeed, these are nurtured and encouraged as we try to live out the gospel message.

Simultaneously with the growth of the church's need for greater numbers of workers with children and youth, there has been an explosion in litigation against the church for incidents of child sexual abuse. Every state now has some statutory requirements in place for the reporting of an incident of child abuse. This, coupled with the blazing attention focused by the media on the child victim and the church, has increased the number of criminal charges against the perpetrators of abuse and the number of civil lawsuits seeking monetary damages for the injuries suffered by the child.

The concept of *"charitable immunity,"* which in the past shielded churches from many types of litigation, no longer serves as a viable protection in cases of child abuse. The public and the courts deem the harm done by child abuse too great to allow such incidents to go unreported and unpunished. Frequently, the punishment comes in the form of monetary damages in huge verdicts against the perpetrator and/or the institution in which the perpetrator worked or volunteered. While a church cannot be the absolute guarantor of the safety of each person within its community and its ministries, it must be recognized that every church can be responsibly attentive to reducing and eliminating circumstances that could in some situations lead to harm or injury.

Recognizing the frequency of the occurrence of child abuse is only part of the task. As a church, we must become knowledgeable about how to recognize indicators of possible abuse, and we must become knowledgeable about how to safely carry out our ministries without providing opportunities for abusers to harm our children.

The church must not look upon the reality of child abuse as a reason to withdraw from its ministries with children! Instead, we must work to assure that our ministries are carried out in responsibly safe circumstances. We, as members of the community of faith, are called to remember the pledge made as each child is baptized. Remembering that, we are called to make the church a safe and holy place where children will be confirmed and strengthened in their faith.

Indicators of Child Abuse

Children suffering abuse often will not tell anyone about it. Therefore, it is important to be able to recognize other signs of abuse. The following characteristics may be indicators of abuse, although they are not necessarily proof. Individually, any one of the indicators may be signs of a number of other more or less serious problems. When these indicators are observed in a child, they can be considered as warnings and lead you to look into the situation further.

Possible Signs of Physical Abuse

1. Hostile and aggressive behavior toward others
2. Fearfulness of parents and/or other adults
3. Destructive behavior toward self, others, and/or property
4. Inexplicable fractures or bruises inappropriate for child's developmental stage
5. Burns, facial injuries, pattern of repetitious bruises

Possible Signs of Emotional Abuse

1. Exhibits severe depression and/or withdrawal
2. Exhibits severe lack of self-esteem
3. Failure to thrive
4. Threatens or attempts suicide
5. Speech and/or eating disorders
6. Goes to extremes to seek adult approval
7. Extreme passive/aggressive behavior patterns

Possible Signs of Neglect

1. Failure to thrive
2. Pattern of inappropriate dress for climate
3. Begs or steals food; chronic hunger
4. Depression
5. Untreated medical conditions
6. Poor hygiene

Possible Signs of Sexual Abuse

1. Unusually advanced sexual knowledge and/or behavior for child's age and developmental stage
2. Depression - cries often for no apparent reason
3. Promiscuous behavior
4. Runs away from home and refuses to return
5. Difficulty walking or sitting
6. Bruised/bleeding in vaginal or anal areas
7. Exhibits frequent headaches, stomachaches, extreme fatigue
8. Sexually transmitted diseases

Notes:

WHO ARE ABUSERS?

Abusers are not easily recognizable—they may look just like you or me! Abusers are people who have greater power in relation to a child, and they use that power to harm the child.

Notes:

In addition to these indicators, children who have been sexually abused at church may exhibit some of the following:

1. Unusual nervousness or anxiety about being left in the nursery or Sunday school class
2. Reluctance to participate in church activities that were previously enthusiastically approached
3. Comments such as "I don't want to be alone with _____" in reference to a childcare worker or Sunday school teacher
4. Nightmares including a childcare worker or teacher as a frightening character
5. Unexplained hostility toward a childcare worker or teacher

Possible Signs of Ritual Abuse

1. Disruptions of memory or consciousness
2. Unexplained mistrust and mood swings
3. Flashbacks
4. Eating disorders
5. Fear of the dark, especially at sundown or a full moon
6. Agitation or despair that seems to occur in cycles
7. Fear of ministers, priests, or others wearing robes or uniforms
8. Nightmares or sleep disorders
9. Any of the symptoms of sexual abuse

Child abuse occurs every minute of every day, and it occurs in every community. Child abuse occurs in every economic, racial, ethnic, religious, or other demographic group. No segment of our society is immune. As Christians, we are called to be vigilant in protecting the children in our midst and in preventing child abuse in the community of faith.

Abusers: Who Are They?

To prevent child abuse in our churches, we must not only recognize the signs of abuse, but we must recognize that the abusers of our children are more often than not familiar adults trusted by the children. Less than twenty percent of child abuse is perpetrated by strangers. In other words, in more than three quarters of the reported incidents of child abuse, the victim was related to or acquainted with the abuser!

Just as children from all segments of our society are victims of child sexual abuse, it is also true that abusers come from all segments of society. Abusers can be found in every racial, ethnic, economic, and social group. When they are

LESS THAN TWENTY PERCENT of child abuse is perpetrated by strangers.

identified, they look very much like us. Some are charismatic leaders; some are very sociable; some are very sympathetic to troubled children; some are married and have children; some are young (even as young as fourteen or fifteen); and some are older adults.

Within our churches, who are the abusers? They may be Sunday school teachers, nursery workers, preschool teachers, children's choir helpers, vacation Bible school leaders, camp counselors, youth group counselors, clergy, or anyone else.

How Does Abuse Happen?

Child sexual abuse happens when a person exerts his or her power over a child in ways that harm and/or exploit the child. In other words, the abuser is powerful; the child is vulnerable. There may be several sources from which the abuser gains power over the child: size, position, knowledge, money, just to name a few. All of these things work to make the abuser believe that he or she is able to behave inappropriately toward a child and that the child will be unable to stop the abusive behavior.

The child is vulnerable to an abuser as a result of having fewer resources available to him or her. The child is physically smaller and weaker, intellectually less mature, and economically dependent upon the abuser or some other adult for sustenance. When a child's vulnerability and an abuser's misuse of power combine with the opportunity to exploit the child without being discovered, then child sexual abuse may and often does occur.

Members of our churches do not like to think that any person in the Sunday school or any other ministry of the church would harm a child. Conversely, we do not like to think that false allegations of abuse could be made by any child in the church. But without a comprehensive strategy against abuse, we are taking a needless risk that harm may be done to our children or our workers with children.

It is imperative for our churches **not** to adopt or implement child abuse prevention policies that apply to only a few categories of people. Strategies must be supported by the whole congregation and carried out by applying the same policies and requirements to each worker involved in children's ministries. When a congregation adopts a child abuse prevention strategy that applies only to the paid nursery workers or only to professional staff members, it

Notes:

WITHOUT A COMPREHENSIVE strategy against abuse, we are taking a needless risk that harm may be done to our children or our workers with children.

Notes:

has adopted a plan that is doomed to be no more than partially successful. It exempts many people from the strategy's requirements and may create specific opportunities for abusers to have unlimited access to our children.

Consequences of Child Sexual Abuse

When one child is sexually abused within our church, many victims are created, including the child, the congregation, the child's family, and often the family of the abuser.

Of foremost importance is the child who has been harmed; he or she must be cared for. Innocence has been stolen from the child. The trauma of abuse may cause emotional injury as well as physical injury, and these scars will last through the victim's life. When child sexual abuse is perpetrated by a trusted person in the church, even greater harm is done to the child's faith in God and faith in the church. The child may struggle with questions like: "If God loves children, how could God have let this happen to me?" and "How can the members of this congregation continue praying and singing week after week, acting as if nothing has happened?" Experiences of abuse in the church create massive obstacles to the child's development of a living, sustaining faith. This consequence is no less important than the physical injuries or the eventual depression, fear, and lack of sufficient self-esteem that often develop as a result of sexual abuse.

The congregation also becomes a victim after abuse is revealed. Members are stunned that such a crime could have been perpetrated within their midst. They are humiliated at their failure to maintain the church as a safe and holy place for children. Members fear that they are ill equipped to help the child's healing process. They are angry that a person welcomed into their fellowship would dare to violate the gospel's mandate by harming a child. Often, members are divided when the congregation begins to think about how to address all of the problems created by the incident.

In addition, the congregation may suffer for a very long time if civil or criminal litigation ensues as a result of the abuse. Litigation in the courts keeps the incident alive for an extended period of time and may make resolution of the emotional issues even more difficult. Over the past decade, litigation involving congregations has become more frequent. As a result, we are finally becoming aware of the

CHILD ABUSE IN THE CHURCH

creates many victims:

-the child

-the child's family

-the congregation

-the family of the abuser

effects of the long, time-consuming, and costly process on the congregation. **Although criminal or civil litigation is often necessary in such situations, the litigation process itself will not provide what is needed for healing among the congregation's members**. For this healing, the community of faith must delve into its biblical foundations and find strength to conquer the evils of fear and to conquer the lack of knowledge about abuse. The congregation must make a renewed commitment to living out the gospel's call to provide and care for children.

Finally, the financial consequences of child sexual abuse in the church cannot be ignored. As reports of abuse and lawsuits increase, the financial costs rise exponentially. A victim of child sexual abuse and his or her family will suffer financially since the costs of counseling and medical treatment go higher each year. A congregation need only ask its insurance agent for the latest statistics to learn that the amounts paid by churches, as settlements or verdicts in abuse cases, can be astronomical—ranging from thousands of dollars to millions.

Currently, no congregation can afford, either financially, ethically, or morally, to fail to implement strategies for the reduction and prevention of child sexual abuse. We, as Christians, are not called to discontinue our congregations' ministries with children and youth. We are called to engage in these ministries with great rejoicing and with the knowledge that we are making every effort to provide ministry to our children and youth in ways that assure their safety while they grow in faith.

Notes:

Recruiting, Screening, and Hiring Workers

WHEN A CONGREGATION decides to develop and implement a comprehensive strategy for the prevention of child sexual abuse, the best place to begin is with the development of appropriate procedures for recruiting, screening, and hiring the people who will work with children and youth. In spite of other adopted safety procedures, if a church does not include a thorough screening process, it will not provide the control and security necessary to assure the safety of children participating in its ministries. Each congregation should approach the recruitment/screening/hiring process in two stages. First, there needs to be a procedure for the employees and volunteers who will work with children and youth on a regular and frequent basis. Second, there needs to be a procedure for workers who will only be involved with children on an occasional basis. By implementing such a system, even workers who are called at the last minute to replace a regular worker can be recruited from a group that has been adequately screened in advance.

From the standpoint of reducing the legal liability of the church if an incident of child abuse occurs, having implemented a thorough screening process for the church's workers with children and youth and having applied that process to all workers (paid and volunteer) will go a long way toward demonstrating that the church has taken reasonable actions to protect its children. When the use of a thorough screening process is coupled with the regular use of additional safety procedures, such as the "Two-Adult Rule"(discussed later in this resource), the reasonableness of the church's actions is further demonstrated. In addition, use of a thorough recruitment and screening process may reduce the risk of false allegations being made against your workers. By making it known to the whole congregation that all workers with children have been carefully selected, indeed "hand picked," for their positions, you are assuring that only workers who will put the children's best interests first have been selected. Thus, people who might consider making false allegations against any of the workers will have the worker's reputation and selection as additional obstacles to overcome in making the allegations credible.

Notes:

_____

_____

_____

_____

_____

_____

_____

_____

_____

_____

IF ANY STRANGER OR NEW
member can have immediate access to our children, we have failed to provide the safe sanctuary we promised our children at their baptism.

Important Forms

The following items should be included in each congregation's recruitment/screening/hiring process for workers with children and youth:

- Position descriptions
- Position application forms
- Personal reference forms
- Consent to criminal background check forms
- Personal interview summary forms

Samples of each of these forms are provided in this resource (pp. 61-76). Please be aware that these are only samples, and you should modify each (in consultation with legal counsel) to meet the requirements of your church as well as the requirements of your state and local laws. The appropriate use of these forms will vary depending upon whether you are recruiting occasional workers or regular workers (both paid and volunteer).

Recruiting Regular Workers

For full-time, part-time, paid, volunteer, clergy, or lay use an application form that requests comprehensive information regarding the applicant's

- identification
- address
- employment history for the past five years
- volunteer work during the past five years
- experiences and skills specifically related to the position
- prior church membership (if any)
- personal references (not related to applicant) with complete addresses
- consent to verify all information provided and to contact the references
- waiver of any right to confidentiality and of any right to pursue damages against the church caused by the reference's response
- certification that the information provided is true and correct

If permitted in your local legal jurisdiction, also request that the applicant list **any** criminal convictions (even traffic violations since workers with children and youth often need to drive church vehicles).

Finally, include a space for the applicant's signature and date.

Reference Check Forms

Forms similar to the sample on page 70 provide the employer with an outline of the information needed from references, as well as a place to note the responses if the contact is being made by telephone. (These forms are also useful if the reference check is conducted through the mail.)

Interviews

A personal interview is not required for every applicant but should certainly be conducted for those the church are seriously considering after reviewing their applications and references. Use the interview to clarify any questions you may have about information on the application and to form a firsthand impression of the applicant. Training for conducting this type of screening interview is often available from agencies such as the YMCA or the Girl Scouts. If it is available in your location, take advantage of it.

Screening Workers

When your church begins to implement the recruiting and screening procedure, it will be necessary to have the appropriate forms completed by workers already working. New applicants should be required to complete the entire procedure before being considered for a position.

Ideally, a recruiting and screening procedure like the one outlined here will be applied to any member of the church staff (paid or volunteer, clergy or lay) who will be involved in work with children and youth. Sometimes the clergy do not recognize the importance of following the procedures. Clergy have been heard to say things like, "Oh, you don't need to check me out. I'm a minister!" Or, "The annual conference board of ministry has already done all this and if the board says I'm good enough for this church, then I don't have to answer any more questions."

Responses like these put the church in an awkward position. The usual result is that the church applies the screening procedures only to non-clergy workers. We certainly hope that the church does not come to regret its choice. Nevertheless, it is necessary to remind churches that allegations of child sexual abuse are brought against clergy as well as laity. If an incident involving a clergyperson who refused to submit to the screening procedure is reported, how will the church respond when the victim's parents cry, "How could you let this so-called 'minister' be involved with our children when he had a criminal record?"

Notes:

BE FIRM AND STEADFAST IN your commitment to careful recruiting, screening, and hiring practices.

Notes:

THE CHURCH'S SCREENING procedures should be equally applied to all workers (paid, volunteer, clergy, lay) who will interact with children and youth.

Even if the church is able to mollify the victim's parents, they may still face staggering consequences if litigation ensues. Beyond the financial consequences, the congregation will be confronted by haunting thoughts of "If only we had stood firm and made Rev. _____ fill out those forms."

If clergy do not cooperate in the screening procedures, they have little defense if false allegations are made against them. Local churches expect that their ministers are of sterling character, and they usually are. Therefore, clergy should not be overly concerned about reference and criminal background checks. Once the responses are on file, the church can prove that it made reasonable efforts to screen staff members and that no reason was discovered that would preclude the person's involvement with children and youth.

In other words, full cooperation with the screening procedure by clergy staff creates a "win - win" situation for the church and the clergy. The church is able to maintain the integrity of its commitment to the prevention of child abuse, and the clergyperson sets a good example for all other staff. In addition, the clergyperson's good character is reinforced by the reports received from his or her references.

Recruiting Occasional Workers

The recruiting/screening procedures outlined for full-time or part-time workers are also ideal for use with workers who may only work a few hours or a few events each year. However, in a local church, it is frequently impossible to use such a procedure when a regular worker cannot come to work and the nursery is short-staffed. Frequently the nursery coordinator appeals to little Joey's mom saying, "We're short a worker today. Could you please stay in the nursery just for the morning worship service?" Usually, Joey's mom is happy to volunteer, and the nursery coordinator's problem is solved. Imagine the consequences if Joey's mom is later accused of abusing a child in the nursery during the time she was there as a volunteer worker. Whether the accusation turns out to be true or false, a crisis is created for the church, for the child and his or her family, and for the volunteer and her family.

How can the local church maintain its commitment to preventing child abuse, including a thorough screening of all workers with children and youth, and still have enough flexibility to recruit last-minute help? One possibility is to create a bank of potential occasional volunteers by introducing the church's policies and procedures to new members in their initial membership orientation.

The new member orientation could include
- a membership form requesting the following information: name, address, church membership during the past three to five years, volunteer work done in previous churches, and two references with addresses (if the new member is not transferring by letter from the previous church). Explain that each new member will be asked to fill out the membership form before he or she is invited to volunteer as a worker with children or youth and that no new members will be invited to volunteer to work with children or youth before they have been members of the church for at least six months.
- a written copy of the church's policies and procedures for the prevention of child abuse.
- a covenant for the member to sign stating that in the event the member is recruited to work with children or youth, he or she agrees to follow the church's policies and procedures for the prevention of child abuse.

By providing these things to each new member, you are giving him or her the opportunity to inform the church of his or her desire to work with children or youth. You are also giving the new member the opportunity to learn the church's policies and to either cooperate with them or decide not to volunteer with children and youth.

This type of new member orientation and screening serves two very important purposes. It helps the congregation identify new members who are willing to volunteer with children and youth, and it very possibly will discourage a potential abuser from any effort to abuse in this congregation. Thus, you have created another "win - win" situation for the children and for the congregation.

Use of Criminal Background Checks

Including the use of criminal background or records checks as a part of the local church's recruiting/screening/hiring process for workers with children and youth is, without a doubt, the most often objected to part of the process. People seeking employment, or people who are simply volunteering to teach Sunday school, may see this as an invasion of their privacy and as an affront to their integrity.

Notes:

SCREENING REDUCES THE RISK OF
- a child abuser being recruited to work with your children.
- your church being accused of negligent hiring practices.
- false allegations being brought against workers.

Notes:

Comments can be expected, including, "I've been a member of this church for fifteen years, and if they don't trust me by now, they can just find someone else to keep the nursery!" Or, "What is this world coming to? All I wanted to do was help with Sunday school. What's the big deal?"

In spite of reactions such as these, criminal background/records checks are becoming a more commonly used screening tool in churches. **Some states now require such inquiries by any organization recruiting workers with children as part of the state's child abuse laws**. Many churches make the decision to include this tool, even if not required by state law, as another way of reducing the probability that a worker has a history of child abuse.

As your church plans its screening procedures, serious consideration must be given to whether you include a background check. Here are some initial questions to consider: Does your state law require its use? Will your local legal jurisdiction assist in the records check? What information is required by the law enforcement agency to perform the records check? **To help your congregation gather the necessary information, it will be useful to consult a local attorney, your church's insurance agent, as well as local law enforcement officers.**

The local church must decide what to do with the information it receives from background reports. A strict plan should be developed to ensure that information will be kept confidential and that it will only be shared with those who must know. Decisions will need to be made as to where the reports will be stored.

If information shows that an applicant was convicted of child abuse, child molestation, incest, or some other crime against a child, that applicant should definitely be rejected as a worker with children or youth. If information indicates that charges were filed against an applicant but that there was no conviction, then the church should investigate how the issue was resolved. Contact the police department or the prosecuting attorney's office to discover more of the details. When the maximum amount of information has been gathered, you will need to make a decision about whether this applicant poses too great a risk to the church's children and youth. Be sure to document in the church's confidential file every step taken during the investigation and the decisions made.

THE SCREENING OF ALL
workers with children and youth, including clergy, creates a win-win situation for the church and the workers.

No amount of resistance, objection, or lack of cooperation should stop a local congregation from developing and implementing comprehensive recruiting/screening/hiring policies and procedures for all its workers—paid or volunteer, clergy or lay, full-time or part-time—with children and youth. If any stranger or new member can have immediate access to our children, the effect of other safety procedures will be limited.

Notes:

Basic Procedures for Safe Ministry with Children and Youth

AFTER A LOCAL CHURCH has made the commitment to take precautions against abuse in its ministries with children and youth, the congregation needs to develop basic procedures to guide the day-to-day operation of its ministries. This can be thought of as the "nuts and bolts" of carrying out the church's ministries with children after the workers are chosen. These procedures are designed to make ministry flow smoothly by reducing the possibility of harm to the children, youth, and the workers. Once again, the procedures will demonstrate to members and visitors alike the church's commitment to the prevention of child abuse and its commitment to being a safe and holy place where children can grow in the faith.

Each of the following procedures is important in the congregation's comprehensive prevention strategy. They are not listed in order of importance.

The "Two-Adult Rule"

Simply stated, the "Two-Adult Rule" requires no fewer than two adults present at all times during any church-sponsored program, event, or ministry involving children. Risk will be reduced even more if the two adults are not related. The nursery is always attended by at least two adults. A Sunday school class for children is always led by at least two adults. A Bible study group for youth is always taught by at least two adults. The youth fellowship group is always staffed with at least two adult counselors/leaders.

The significance of this rule cannot be overstated. A church will drastically reduce the possibility of an incident of child abuse if this rule is followed. **Abusers thrive on secrecy, isolation, and their ability to manipulate victims. When abusers know they will never have a chance to be alone with potential victims, they quickly lose interest in "working" with the children.** Thus, the children are protected, and the church has greatly reduced the likelihood of a claim of child abuse. Furthermore, vigilant adherence to the "Two-Adult Rule" provides important protection to the church's workers with children and youth. Even small churches can adhere to this rule by

Notes:

using assigned adult "roamers" who move in and out of rooms. Parents and children who know that two adults will be present at all times are less likely to make false allegations; they know that it would be nearly impossible to prove allegations against two workers. Church members will be more confident when they volunteer to work with children, knowing that they will never bear the total burden of leadership and knowing that the church has made a commitment to protecting them as well as the children.

First Aid/CPR Training

Providing first aid and CPR training on an annual basis for all church workers with children and youth is a basic step to assure the safety of children. It is hoped that first aid or CPR would never be needed in the church. Nevertheless, ministries with children and youth inevitably involve activities that can result in bumps, bruises, and scrapes. Having workers who are prepared to deal with these competently goes a long way toward building the confidence of the children and the parents involved in the ministry of the church.

Annual Orientation for Workers

All workers with children and youth, whether the workers are paid, volunteer, part-time, full-time, clergy, or lay, should be required to attend an orientation session in which they are informed of the

- church's policies for the prevention of child abuse.
- procedures to be used in all ministries with children and youth.
- appropriate steps to report an incident of child abuse.
- details of the state laws regarding child abuse.

At this orientation the workers are given an opportunity to renew their covenant to abide by and cooperate with the church's policies and procedures. The church will have an updated record that it has informed all of its workers about its policies. Workers who do not attend should be contacted and asked to renew the covenant.

The "Five-Years-Older" Rule

Often, especially in youth ministry, the people who volunteer to work or who apply for a paid position are in college or have just graduated. If a junior in college (age 20 or 21) is recruited to serve as a counselor in the senior-high youth fellowship, the counselor may be "leading" youth who are only three or four years younger than he or she is. This should be

A CHURCH WILL DRASTICALLY reduce the possibility of an incident of child abuse by following the "Two-Adult" rule.

prohibited for the protection of the youth and the worker. Nearly every church has members who can remember a situation in which this rule was not followed and the persons involved came to regret it. Do not make the same mistake.

No Workers under the Age of Eighteen

When a church implements this rule it goes a long way toward reducing the risks of injuries to its children and youth. A very common practice in churches is to allow junior- and senior-high aged volunteers in the church nursery. In effect, the church is using children to supervise children. While in some situations they may provide excellent help, people under the age of eighteen cannot be expected to have developed the maturity and judgment that is needed to be fully responsible for younger children. **Putting children in charge of children invites disaster.**

Windows in All Classroom Doors

Each room set aside for children and youth should have a door with a window in it or a half door. A window in every door removes the opportunity for secrecy and isolation, conditions every child abuser seeks. A half door offers protection against children wandering outside the classroom and allows for full visual access. Many pastors are adding a window in their study or office door to set a good example for the church and to protect themselves against false allegations of misconduct.

Open-Door Counseling

At any counseling sessions with children or youth, the door of the room used should remain open for the entire session. Ideally, the session will be conducted at a time when others are nearby, even if they are not within listening distance. Counseling sessions conducted behind closed doors are a breeding ground for false allegations of abuse. Closed doors also make it too easy for the child abuser to have the privacy and isolation he or she needs.

Advance Notice to Parents

A basic rule for ministry with children and youth is to **always** give the parents advance notice and full information regarding the event(s) in which their children will be participating. Risk management officers advise clients to notify parents of any event in which a worker will be alone with a child. Before the event, parents must give written permission for their child's participation. Doing this protects the church

A WINDOW IN EVERY DOOR removes the opportunity for secrecy and isolation, conditions every child abuser seeks.

Notes:

in that it proves that parents were informed of the event, warned of the situation, and given the chance to prevent their child from being alone with a worker.

Providing parents with advance notice and full information about activities must be a guiding principle in a church's ministries with children and youth. Advance information encourages parents to support the ministry by scheduling their child's participation. It could also possibly lead to parents participating in the ministry as volunteer leaders. Advance information can help parents and children decide whether the content and substance of the event are suitable for their participation. Most importantly, advance information demonstrates that the church takes its ministries seriously enough to plan thoroughly and to provide for the safest possible experiences.

Participation Covenant for All Participants and Leaders

A written covenant of participation should be developed and provided to all leaders and participants in children's and youth ministries. The covenant is a statement in which the participants and leaders agree to
- take part in the ministry.
- give their best efforts to the ministry.
- respect the other participants.
- treat the others as well as they would wish to be treated.

Such covenants are useful (especially for retreats or trips) for establishing from the outset the behavior standards expected of everyone. The covenants are also important reminders for leaders that abusive behavior toward the children and/or youth will not be tolerated.

Parent and Family Education

When a church has made a serious commitment to a comprehensive plan for the prevention of child abuse within its ministries, it will want to provide information about the plan to the congregation and parents. A family education event, or a series of events, in which families are invited to learn the facts about child sexual abuse and about the components of the church's plan is highly effective in disseminating full information to the maximum number of people in a minimal amount of time. An event of this type could include:
- a speaker from your local law enforcement agency.
- a speaker from a local child protective services agency.

PROVIDING PARENTS WITH
advanced notice and full information about activities must be a guiding principle in a church's ministries with children and youth.

- a doctor or counselor who is experienced in treating abused children.
- an attorney experienced in advising churches about risk management or loss prevention.
- a video about the incidence of child sexual abuse within churches.
- printed information about your state's abuse statutes and abuse reporting requirements.
- printed copies of your church's abuse prevention policies and procedures. (Allow time for discussion.)
- a time for worship and prayer.

An event can also include sessions for children so that they are informed about the behavior that is to be expected from other participants and from church leaders, about how to recognize and report possible abuse, and about how they can help prevent harm being done to anyone at the church.

In a church committed to the prevention of child abuse, this event will be provided regularly to accommodate new members and new parents.

Appropriate Equipment and Supervision

Ministries with children and youth are carried out in an endless variety of settings and locations: church sanctuaries, classrooms, camp cabins, playgrounds, retreat centers, tour buses, parks, and homes. Reports of child abuse indicate that abuse happens in an equally large variety of settings. One aspect of planning for the safety of the children and youth participants is arranging for the ministry to take place in an appropriate setting. For instance, if the purpose of the ministry is weekly Bible study, then an appropriate setting would be a classroom at the church. If the purpose of the ministry is for the youth choir to travel for two weeks performing a musical in a dozen different cities, then the settings may include a tour bus, a series of hotel rooms, and a series of church sanctuaries.

The likelihood of the occurrence of child abuse varies in different settings and circumstances. Bible study done in an open-doored classroom and in the presence of no fewer than two adults has a very low probability of an incident happening. However, inadequate supervision of a youth choir at a hotel may increase the odds of an abuse incident. It is very important for those planning ministries with children and youth to think through, in advance, the advantages and disadvantages of the settings they are considering.

PLANNING FOR THEIR physical safety is a necessary part of your ministry with children.

Notes:

_____

_____

_____

_____

_____

_____

_____

_____

_____

_____

Ministries with children and youth often involve using special equipment, and <u>workers should be well aware of how to safely operate whatever equipment is needed</u>. If the ministry involves the use of the church playground, then the workers should know how each piece of play equipment is to be used. When children are on the playground, an adequate number of adults should be with them at all times. Too often stories are told about abuse that occurred on a playground when only one adult (the abuser) was present and had a brief opportunity to isolate the victim out of the sight of anyone else. Incredible as it may seem, children are sometimes left totally unattended on the playground while a dinner or some other event goes on in the church's fellowship hall. A complete stranger can take advantage of the situation to hurt a child, or a child can fall and break an arm without a single adult present to see what happened or to attend to the injury. Both of these situations can lead to nightmarish legal consequences for the church. Do not let your church take this risk.

Other outdoor ministries would involve the need for specialized knowledge. Swimming or rafting events need a supervisor with lifeguard skills. First aid and CPR skills are needed when the ministry involves camping, hiking, and service projects such as Habitat for Humanity or the Appalachian Service Project.

Adequate Insurance for the Scope of Your Ministries

Every local church needs to develop a good relationship with its insurance agent. The church needs to be <u>adequately insured</u> for the scope of its ministry. If the church is *never* involved in ministries that involve transporting people in motor vehicles, then perhaps it can afford not to carry insurance for such occasions. This is very unlikely, just as it is very unlikely that a local church will never be involved with children in any way. Congregations, through their boards of trustees, should very carefully consider all ministries and work with insurance agents to secure adequate coverage for their ministries. Each local church that has adopted a plan for the prevention of child abuse will be well ahead in the task of securing economical insurance coverage. If the church has not developed a plan for the prevention of child abuse, the insurance agent will be a valuable resource in supplying up-to-date information about the risks associated with child abuse in churches.

Developing a Congregational Plan for Responding to Allegations of Abuse

THE CONGREGATION'S plan for responding to suspected or alleged incidents of child abuse must be developed long before it may be needed. Two key components must be included in the plan: First, review your state's law for requirements in reporting suspected or known child abuse to child protective services or to the local police. Second, develop a plan for complying with the legal reporting requirements and for making statements to other officials and the media.

State Reporting Requirements

All workers with children and youth must know their state's requirements in reporting abuse to law enforcement authorities and child protective services. Each state has specific requirements, and you should consult a local attorney about what requirements are applicable to the workers in your church.

In some states, all childcare workers—either paid or volunteer—are mandated to report suspected cases of child abuse when they have reasonable cause. However, this is not true in every state. It is imperative to know what your state requires. In some states, ordained ministers are not mandatory reporters, even if they are appointed to work as "ministers to children and families" or "ministers of children's programming." Instead, they are considered "permissive reporters" and are simply encouraged to report when they have reasonable cause to believe that abuse has occurred.

Some states provide for reports to be made anonymously while others do not. If your state allows anonymous reports, it is advisable to take the precaution of making the report by telephone in the presence of an objective witness, such as the church pastor or the church's attorney, who can verify that the report was made and by whom in case this is needed later. Many

Notes:

states provide immunity for those making reports of child abuse in good faith—meaning that the accused cannot bring a lawsuit against the reporter as long as the person had reasonable cause to believe that abuse had occurred.

Every state has statutory definitions of child abuse and child sexual abuse. Workers with children must know these definitions to recognize whether or not the behavior they believe may be abusive meets the statutory definition. A local attorney, or the church's insurance agent, should be consulted to get the current definitions for your state.

Every state's child abuse statutes include a reporting time limit. Once a person becomes aware of or suspects abuse, he or she must report it to the proper authorities within a set amount of time. Workers with children and youth must be familiar with this deadline to comply. In some states it is as short as twenty-four hours. Workers with children and youth may also be subject to criminal penalties, by the requirements of state statutes, for failure to make appropriate and timely reports. Therefore, it is imperative that they be informed of these requirements. Workers must know the correct agencies to which they can report abuse. If state law requires that the local sheriff's department be contacted, and the childcare worker simply mentions her suspicions of abuse to the nursery coordinator, then a proper report has not been made under the requirements of state law.

Obviously, it is important to gather accurate information about your state's current child abuse statutes before developing the church's reporting procedures. Contact the church's attorney, another local attorney, the local child protective services agency, or your church's insurance agent for help in gathering up-to-date information. Draft a step-by-step plan for reporting any incident of actual or suspected abuse.

At this point, it will be necessary and important to educate and train all of the church's workers with children and youth so that they are fully aware of their responsibilities under state law and under the church's prevention policies. Ideally, this education event should include the entire clergy and lay staff of the church, all full-time, part-time, paid or volunteer workers, all parents of children and youth, and any others who are interested. Parents need to know that the people caring for their children at the church are well informed and capable of taking appropriate actions in the event of suspected or alleged child abuse.

EVERY CHURCH IS AT RISK
if it engages in ministry with children in any way.

Clergy staff members, even if they are "permissive reporters" under state law, need to be informed of the law's requirements. I cannot overstate this: Workers must be fully informed to be able to make lawful reports and to avoid possible criminal penalties for failure to report.

Beyond the State's Requirements

The church's commitment to the prevention of child abuse requires that its workers with children and youth make reports of abuse according to the requirements of state law. However, our obligations to respond to allegations go beyond the requirements of state law. As Christians, we must also be prepared to respond to others regarding allegations of abuse. We must be prepared to respond to the victim and his or her family, to the news media, to our church's insurance agent, to the annual conference, and possibly to the abuser.

Faithful response to the victim will include taking the allegation very seriously and respecting the victim's privacy, as well as providing sympathetic concern for the victim and his or her family. Faithful response to the victim does not condone blaming the victim or implying that the victim was in any way responsible for causing the abuse.

Faithful response to the annual conference will include notifying conference authorities (the church's district superintendent or the resident bishop) as soon as allegations of abuse are received. Conference authorities must be kept aware of the congregation's actions throughout the process up to the resolution. It will also be necessary to notify the church's insurance agent if an allegation of child abuse is made.

Faithful response to the media can be one of the most frightening needs for a local church. However, it can be accomplished fairly simply. In advance, designate one person who will speak to the media. This person may be the pastor, another staff member, the church's attorney, or a lay member of the church, such as the chairman of the board of trustees. The person chosen should be capable of speaking calmly and thoughtfully in the glare of cameras and microphones. This person should answer questions honestly without adding extra or unnecessary information. **The designated spokesperson should be given permission to answer questions by saying, "I (we) don't know at this time." None but the spokesperson should be authorized to speak to the media on behalf of the congregation.**

Notes:

KNOW THE LEGAL REPORTING requirements for your state. Get up-to-date information from your church's attorney or insurance agent.

Notes:

KNOW YOUR STATE'S
definition of child abuse and child sexual abuse.

The designated spokesperson should be prepared to state the church's policy for the prevention of child abuse, the church's concern for the safety of the victim and all children, and the procedures the church has followed to reduce the risk of abuse to children. Speaking extemporaneously is tempting in situations such as this, but it is ill advised. The designated spokesperson will do well to have a prepared statement, or at least to have written notes so that the church's policies and procedures can be set forth very clearly. The designated spokesperson should never make any statements indicating that the church fails to take this allegation seriously or that the church suspects the victim has "just made up this little story to get attention."

Faithful response to the accused abuser will include acknowledging that he or she is a person of sacred worth; but a faithful response will also acknowledge that the accused must stop the abusive behavior, prayerfully repent and turn in a new direction. Faithful response will include removing the accused from his or her position as a worker with children and youth until the allegations are fully investigated and resolved; it does not necessarily mean that the accused will at some future time be placed again in a position of trust involving children and youth. Finally, faithful response does not include forgiving the accused before justice is achieved and the victim is ready to contemplate forgiveness.

Not "If It Happens" but "When It Happens"
Since child abuse happens every fifteen seconds and in any location, it is not so unimaginable that a church could be called upon to respond to an allegation of abuse. The local church that has made a commitment to the prevention of child abuse is well on its way to being able to respond faithfully and effectively.

In a nutshell, when an allegation of child abuse is made against a worker or member, be prepared to do the following:
- Notify the parents of the victim, and take any necessary steps to assure the child's safety until the parents arrive. **The safety of the victim must be the church's primary concern.**
- Do not confront the accused abuser with anger and hostility. Treat him or her with dignity, but immediately remove him or her from further involvement with children or youth.

- Notify the proper law enforcement or child protective services agency.
- Notify the annual conference authorities, the church's insurance agent, and the church's attorney.
- Keep a written record of the steps taken by the church in response.
- Call upon your designated spokesperson to make any necessary statements or responses to the news media.
- Prepare a brief and honest statement that can be made to the congregation **without giving unnecessary details, placing blame, interfering with the victim's privacy, or violating any confidentiality concerns.**
- Be prepared to cooperate fully with the investigation conducted by law enforcement officials or child protective services.

When a local church receives a report or allegation of child abuse against a person who has been trusted with the care and nurture of its children, it is immediately a crisis situation. The best and most faithful response is one that is planned in advance. By careful and thoughtful preparation, the congregation can provide a greater measure of love and concern for the victim and others involved while also cooperating, as necessary, with local authorities. Plan ahead to preserve your congregation's ability to surround the children with steadfast love and establish them in the faith.

Notes:

Implementation Strategies for the Congregation

FOR A CHILD ABUSE prevention policy to be successful, the entire congregation must wholeheartedly support its adoption and implementation. Universal support will not happen without a thorough and comprehensive plan for educating the congregation and for including a wide spectrum of members in the development of the policy and procedures.

The formation of a committee or task force to prepare the policy should be a result of careful consideration. Whoever has responsibility for naming the membership of the task force (church council, council on ministries, administrative board) should invite representatives from any group that engages in ministry with children and youth: Sunday school teachers, fellowship leaders, nursery workers, preschool workers, daycare workers, music ministry leaders. Parents and grandparents of children in preschool, elementary, middle-high and senior-high grade levels should also be invited because they can make valuable contributions. By forming an inclusive task force you will reduce the likelihood of creating policies and procedures that will engender serious opposition from segments of the congregation. Instead, concerns can be brought to the task force and dealt with while the policy is still being developed.

As soon as the task force is named, it must meet and begin its work. Start by scheduling a series of at least six meetings. Set your meetings according to the projected completion date of the policy. Plan for each meeting to last approximately ninety minutes. There are several things that the task force will need to accomplish. These tasks include the following:

- Research issues related to child abuse.
- Evaluate the current practices of your church related to the care and supervision of children and youth.
- Develop new policies and procedures for the care and supervision of children and youth.
- Develop a plan for responding to allegations of child abuse.
- Develop a plan for responding to known incidents of child abuse.

Notes:

A COMPREHENSIVE PLAN HAS

- screening and training procedures for workers with children and youth
- reporting procedures for allegations of abuse
- a process for responding to allegations of abuse

- Present new policies and procedures to the church council or other approving body.
- Plan to educate the congregation about abuse and the new prevention policies.
- Plan training and periodic refresher training about the new policies for all church workers with children and youth.
- Celebrate!

Task 1:
Research issues related to child abuse.

For the task force to effectively develop policies and procedures related to child abuse, it must have a solid foundation in basic information about abuse. Without this foundation the process of creating a prevention policy will be far more difficult, if not impossible. Some of this information could be provided to the task force in writing before the meeting, but plan substantial group discussion time. Steps in completing this task should include the following:

1. Review the definition and types of child abuse, using information from pages 12-13.

2. Review the statistics of the frequency of child abuse (p. 15).

3. Ask the members to think back over the past few weeks and recall incidents of child abuse in your community.

4. Have the members list the places and settings in which child abuse could occur in your congregation, such as: Sunday school, youth fellowship, youth choir, children's choir, other youth serving groups that meet in the church (Girl Scouts, Boy Scouts, and so forth), preschool/daycare, vacation Bible school, summer sports camps, and other ministries specific to your congregation.

5. Explore the question, "Who are the victims of child abuse?" Children and youth who are vulnerable as a result of being smaller, weaker, more isolated, or more trusting of adults are potential victims. (See p. 19 for more information.)

6. Explore the question, "Who are the abusers?" Abusers cannot be neatly stereotyped. Almost anyone can be an abuser under certain circumstances. There is no

single personality type that is likely to become an abuser. There is currently no psychological test or tool that can accurately predict which person is, or will be, a child abuser. (See pp. 18-19 for more information.) It may be helpful for the task force to invite a resource person (such as a parish attorney or a representative of the local child protective services) to the meeting to present current information about abuse and abusers.

7. Explore the range of frequent reactions from abusers. These include denial, minimization, blame, anger, threats, and manipulation. Task force members, as well as congregation members, need to recognize the typical reactions. When child abuse happens and the abuser is confronted, any or all of these reactions may be displayed and may be very persuasive.

8. Review the consequences of child abuse in the church. The range of consequences include: psychological harm and/or injury to the victim; trauma and distress in the victim's family and the congregation; distress in the abuser's family; and possible legal damages and/or verdicts against the church.

Task 2:
Evaluate the current practices of your church related to the care and supervision of children and youth.

1. Explore the circumstances and situations in the church that could make it easier for an abuser to hurt a child. These could include inadequate recruiting and screening policies and practices for hiring workers with children and youth, inadequate supervision of workers, and inadequate control of workers and ministry settings, including a lack of observation and/or evaluation of the workers. Even if your church utilizes only volunteer workers with children and youth, there must be adequate supervision and evaluation to assure that ministry is being accomplished safely. When the task force members have identified the circumstances that make abuse possible, they will be better able to understand and identify the ways that abuse can be prevented. Then the task force can move on to developing and integrating a comprehensive prevention policy.

2. Identify current policies. Even if there is no written policy, your church is undoubtedly operating under a

Notes:

EVERY CONGREGATION IS capable of assuring that its church building is a place of security and peace for children!

Notes:

FAITHFUL RESPONSE TO THE
victim will include
-taking the allegations seriously.
-respecting the victim's privacy.
-assuring the victim's safety.

set of unwritten rules that the members simply understand to be "the way things are done." For instance, if your church has no written policy regarding the supervision of youth on a summer mission trip, there is likely an understanding among the parents, youth, and workers about who can serve as chaperones for the trip and how many will be needed. The task force needs to identify the current practices of the church, whether written or unwritten, and begin to decide which are adequate, inadequate, and/or in need of modification.

3. Review the current policies regarding the recruitment and screening of workers with children and youth, including paid workers, volunteers, and clergy staff members. Review the current policies related to training workers regarding child abuse and how to report allegations and/or incidents. Review the policies for supervising workers with children and youth. Review the current practices of how children and/or youth are disciplined to determine whether the methods used are appropriate and whether corporal punishment is excluded. Review the facilities used for ministries with children and youth to determine whether they are suitable. For instance, are the facilities too isolated from the rest of the church? These facilities should not be isolated but should provide openness and visibility for the participants—as well as for the parents coming to pick up their children.

Task 3:
Develop new policies and procedures for the care and supervision of children and youth.
At this point, the group will begin to integrate what it has learned about child abuse and the current circumstances in the congregation. As the new policies are developed, the following practical components need to be considered:
- recruitment and screening practices
- applications
- references
- disclosure forms
- background checks/consent forms
- covenant statements
- use of appropriate facilities for ministries with children and youth
- appropriate types of discipline for children and youth

The sample forms on pages 61-76 will be helpful as the task force develops recruiting and screening forms tailored to the specific circumstances of your congregation. Since the task force will probably not be an ongoing group, it is also important to identify which group in the church will be responsible for the periodic review and updating of the policies and procedures.

Task 4:
Develop a plan for responding to allegations of child abuse.
Even though the task force has drafted child abuse prevention policies and procedures related to the recruitment, screening, and selection of workers, it must include a plan for responding to allegations of abuse if they occur. The primary goal must always be to protect the victim.

Furthermore, any plan designed for your congregation must comply with the laws of your state and local jurisdiction. This resource provides helpful ideas, but it cannot substitute for a consultation with your parish attorney or a local attorney familiar with the current requirements for reporting allegations of child abuse. It would be appropriate to invite a resource person to meet with the task force or to request a written copy of the state laws about reporting requirements.

In addition, your response plan should designate a person (or several people) who will receive reports of abuse in the congregation and follow through on them, according to the requirements of your state law. This can be a clergy staff person, a Sunday school volunteer, or anyone else who is trusted. However, it must be someone who will honor the confidentiality of the reports. When a report or an allegation of abuse is received, these people must be prepared to follow the response plan. They need to remember that, generally, children do not lie about abuse. However, they also need to be aware that false allegations can be made, especially in circumstances involving custody battles. Knowledge about child abuse and familiarity with the children and families of the congregation are important resources for the person receiving the report of abuse.

Your plan should also designate a person who will be responsible for any necessary communication with the media. This does not have to be the senior pastor. It can be any person who is capable of answering questions under pressure. Take care to designate only one person for this responsibility.

Notes:

FAITHFUL RESPONSE TO THE news media includes honest answers, even if that can only be, "We don't know."

47

FAITHFUL RESPONSE TO THE annual conference includes notifying conference authorities as soon as allegations of abuse are received.

Be prepared to keep adequate documentation of any allegations of abuse. Keep incident report forms readily available. Sample forms can be found on page 72-73. The information on the form **must be kept confidential and limited to only those who must know**, such as the legal authorities specified by your state law, the pastor, the district superintendent, the bishop, the church's insurance agent, the parish attorney, and possibly the chair of the staff-parish relations committee. Plan carefully who will have access to the forms and where they will be stored. It is advisable to keep records in a locked file. Emphasize the necessity of documenting all actions and conversations related to allegations.

Task 5:
Develop a plan for responding to known incidents of child abuse.
These steps will be very similar to those for responding to allegations of child abuse. However, several additional components are necessary. Appropriate response to a known incident must include a plan for providing emergency care for the victim; a plan for notifying parents as well as legal authorities; a plan for protecting evidence; a plan for communicating with the media; a process for documenting every action taken and every report made; a plan for removing the abuser from any further contact with children; a plan for enlisting the full cooperation of the church staff; and a plan providing pastoral care to the victim and his or her family. Your congregation may also wish to include a plan for providing pastoral care for the family of the abuser. In some situations this may be more appropriately handled through a minister from a nearby church.

Task 6:
Present new policies and procedures to the church council or other approving body.
When the task force has drafted the policies and procedures outlined above, it will be ready to present its work to the church council or other approving body for endorsement and adoption. Ideally, the task force will have made regular progress reports and given the church council educational information regarding all of the issues related to child abuse prevention. Include in the presentation information about which group in the church will be responsible for periodic reviews of the policies and procedures.

Task 7:
Plan for educating the congregation about abuse and the new prevention policies.

This will be a shared responsibility of the task force and the church council. Educating the membership about abuse and the new policies cannot be accomplished in one meeting of the church council, or in one letter to parents, or in one article in the church newsletter. In developing these policies the members of the task force will come to understand how difficult it is to consider child sexual abuse. Comprehension of the harm caused by the abuse does not come through one committee meeting. Similarly, full understanding as to how abuse can be prevented also takes time. The church council and the task force will be far more successful in reaching full support among the membership if they work together to inform the congregation, over time, about the pertinent issues and the plans being developed for prevention. Remember that people are more apt to respond to information that is presented in a variety of ways. Educate the membership through parent meetings, Sunday school classes, youth fellowship orientation and training meetings, newsletter articles, church bulletin inserts, video presentations, spoken words from the pulpit during worship, and letters from the task force.

Task 8:
Plan training and refresher courses about the new policies for all church workers with children and youth.

An initial orientation and training of all workers with children and youth should include information about the nature of child abuse and its consequences, ways to prevent abuse, and ways to respond to abuse. The training should also educate the workers about the church's new abuse prevention policies and the plan for implementing the policies. A suggested training plan is provided in Chapter Seven. Finally, the task force and the church council will need to designate a group in the church that will be responsible for providing ongoing training and orientation during the year for new workers with children and youth.

Task 9:
Celebrate!

A brief review of this chapter makes it plain that the implementation of a child sexual abuse prevention plan in your congregation will not be accomplished with one brief meeting and vote. The people who accept the invitation to serve on the task force developing the abuse prevention plan will

Notes:

FAITHFUL RESPONSE TO THE accused abuser includes acknowledgment that he or she is a person of sacred worth in need of repentance.

Notes:

be making a sizable commitment of time and energy. When their work is complete and your congregation has adopted a plan, there should be a great celebration!

Plan a time of commitment and rejoicing for the Sunday morning worship services and follow the worship with a celebration luncheon for the entire congregation. Use special music, banners, leaders, and plenty of children and youth to create the celebration. Give special recognition to the task force members, and express the congregation's gratitude for the work they have done. Focus the celebration on the congregational commitment to make your church a sacred and safe place in which all can encounter the love and saving grace of our Lord, Jesus Christ. A suggested order of worship is found on pages 77-78.

A Model for Training Workers

IMPLEMENTING A comprehensive strategy for the prevention of child abuse in a local church cannot be done without a substantial amount of education being provided for the workers with children and youth, the parents of children and youth, the congregation, and the children and youth themselves. This model is designed to be used with your church's workers with children and youth, but you may easily modify it for use with other groups. This model is designed to be used as a three- or a four-hour workshop.

I. Opening Worship

A. Prayer of Invocation

Gracious and most merciful God, you have brought us together in witness to your love of all children. Open our hearts and minds in this moment and prepare us to receive your message. Show us your will and fill us to overflowing with courage to face the reality of child abuse. Give us energy and dedication enough to make this, your church, a holy and hallowed place where all your children may be safe and secure as they grow in faith and in their knowledge of your presence in their lives! Amen.

B. Suggested Scriptures

1. Exodus 22:21-23
2. Matthew 19:14
3. Luke 9:46-48

C. Brief Devotion

You may begin by recalling the baptismal ritual for children, reminding the participants of the pledge made by the congregation at each child's baptism. Acknowledge and list the many ways your congregation lives out that pledge through its current ministries with children. Conclude by introducing the child abuse prevention strategy as the newest component of your church's ministries with children and youth.

Notes:

EDUCATION AND TRAINING
are essential for the successful implementation of policies and procedures to reduce the risk of abuse.

II. Introductory Information

A. Current Occurrences

Set the stage here for the substance of the event by introducing recent news reports from your own community's newspapers or television broadcasts related to incidents of child abuse in any locations and institutions. Also, in this section, present the material related to any current litigation involving the church and claims of child abuse.

B. Current Statistics

Quote the statistical information from this resource or from other sources available to you. Work the math on a chalkboard or newsprint to show how two million annual incidents finally translate into one incident of abuse every fifteen seconds.

C. Reasons to Implement a Child Abuse Prevention Strategy

1. Our church is a community of faith that can offer a safe haven and sanctuary where children and youth can seek advice, help, and nurture.

2. Our church is a place where more than just facts of child abuse can be taught. We can also teach and proclaim our Christian values: compassion, justice, repentance, and grace.

3. Our church is the place where children can come and learn and develop the inner strength and spiritual resources they will need to feel truly connected to God and to face suffering and evil.

4. Our church can be the place where children and adults are able to learn how to respond to painful and confusing events using the wisdom of the Scriptures.

D. Summarize

These reports and data demonstrate that we cannot ignore the possibility that abuse could happen here. For the sake of our children and the protection of our workers against false allegations, we need to intentionally work to prevent abuse.

III. What is Abuse and How Can We Recognize It?

Use the information on pages 12-13 to give definitions and indicators.

A. Physical abuse
B. Emotional abuse
C. Neglect

D. Sexual abuse

E. Ritual abuse

IV. Who Are Abusers? The Balance of Power

Use the information and examples provided on pages 18-20. Discuss the concepts of power and vulnerability and how these can lead to abuse. Use the news reports you shared earlier to help demonstrate the balance-of-power concept. In each account, have the participants list the sources of power available to the abuser. Then have the participants identify the factors that made the child vulnerable to the abuser.

If time allows, you may use a video here to illustrate the concepts you have just addressed. The bibliography and resource list at the end of this book provide suggestions of appropriate videos or sources for videos.

V. What Are We Doing to Keep Our Children and Workers Safe?

Present the new policies and procedures for the prevention of child abuse. Give participants time to read the policies. Allow time for questions and discussion as you review each section with the group.

A. Screening of Staff: Employees and Volunteers

Use your policies and the information in this resource for the substance of this section. Provide copies of all screening forms, application forms, covenant forms, consent forms, and position description forms. Allow time for a review of each form and for questions from the participants.

B. Training of Staff: Employees and Volunteers

Use your policies and the information in this resource for the substance of this section. Be thorough in reviewing all of the safety procedures, and allow time for questions.

C. Reporting Suspected Abuse

Use your policies and the information in this resource to explain the reporting procedure developed for your church. Explain the policy, the procedure for making a report, and the concept of confidentiality.

D. Completing the Task

If this is the first occasion the workers have had to see and review the screening, application, and position description forms, you may need to allow time for each of them to complete a form.

Notes:

HELP WORKERS WITH

children understand that the policies are to protect the workers as well as the children.

Notes:

VI. Closing Worship

A. Covenant Forms

Have one or two people distribute covenant forms to the participants. Say, "We have reached the end of our time together today. Let's prepare to celebrate our church's commitment to protecting our children, youth, and those who work with them. Please read the covenant you have just received, and sign it as your commitment to our church's ministry with children and youth."

B. Return to the Scripture reading from opening worship. Read aloud the verses from Luke 9:46-48.

C. Invite the participants to pray responsively with you by saying, after each sentence prayer, "We welcome the children!"

Leader: O God, by our presence here today,
People: *We welcome the children!*

Leader: O God, by our promise in Holy Baptism,
People: *We welcome the children!*

Leader: O God, by our participation in the ministries of this congregation,
People: *We welcome the children!*

Leader: O God, by our commitment to keeping this place holy and safe in every way,
People: *We welcome the children!*

Leader: O God, give us wisdom, strength, and courage enough to show the world that
People: *We welcome the children!*

All: *Amen!*

D. Offering

Ask the participants to bring forward their signed covenant forms as a sign of offering themselves in ministry with children and youth. Sing the Doxology.

E. Benediction

May the grace of the Lord Jesus Christ, the love of God, and the power of the Holy Spirit guide and direct you in all you do. Amen.

After Abuse, Then What?

chapter eight

WHEN THE ABUSE of a child or youth occurs in the church, there are many victims in addition to the one who has been physically harmed, and all are in need of healing ministry. Who are the other victims?

The other victims may include the
- family members of the child who was harmed.
- peers of the child.
- peers of the child's parents.
- remaining workers with children and youth.
- congregation as a community of faith.
- family of the accused abuser.

Each victim will certainly need to be included in a ministry of comfort and healing.

Child abuse, either within the church or outside of the church, is not a new phenomenon. It has existed for longer than we can remember. What is a relatively new phenomenon is our recognition that the harm of child abuse is exponentially magnified when it is kept secret within the church. Abuse that is hidden continues to cause anger, confusion, and fear in the congregation for years to come. I know of one congregation in which a child was abused by an adult parishioner twenty-seven years ago, and to this day the real truth has not been shared with the whole congregation. As a result, the congregation has been paralyzed by feelings of anger and fear that have existed for so long now that many members cannot even verbalize the reason for the existence of these feelings. The congregation has a reputation among ministers for being an extremely depressing and difficult place to serve. In its local community, the congregation has a reputation of being an unfriendly and unwelcoming group of people. Clearly, failure to address the issues of anger, fear, and grief that occur within the church after abuse can have far-reaching and devastating consequences for everyone.

Notes:

FAILURE TO ADDRESS THE issues of anger, fear, and grief that occur within the church after abuse can have far-reaching and devastating consequences.

How then can your church be in ministry to all, or any, of the victims of child abuse? The reality of ministry after abuse is that it must be aimed at assuring justice for all and healing for those who are suffering. Neither justice nor healing can be achieved in a short time. Just as your congregation has probably spent a year developing its child abuse prevention policy and implementation strategy, it may spend a year or more working toward healing and justice after abuse actually occurs. There is not a workshop to sponsor, or a video to watch, or a speech to make that can create the measure of understanding needed for healing and for justice to be achieved. Ministry with victims, both the individual and the congregation, is very similar to ministry with those in grief. By thinking in those terms, you can begin to grasp the length of time needed for the victim(s) and the congregation as a whole to be restored to a feeling of health and justice.

The First Step

The first step in ministry with victims of child abuse in a congregation must be truth telling. This means engaging in honest communication about what has happened. Truth telling does not mean engaging in gossip or speculation. Above all, truth telling does not mean blaming the child victim in any way!

How will you engage in honest communication? Follow the procedures you have already planned for reporting an incident of abuse to law enforcement authorities and denominational officials. By the time you have done that, it is very likely that rumors will have begun to spread among the members of the congregation. At this point, it is important to provide honest and forthright information. This may begin with a letter to the members that briefly explains the incident and the initial action taken by the church. Such a letter should not include the identification of the child victim nor that of the accused abuser. On the other hand, it should include a statement of the actions taken to assure the safety of all the children and to assure your congregation's continuing ability to provide ministry to children and youth. This letter should dispel rumors and innuendo and assure everyone that everything possible has been done to provide for the safety of the victim(s) and to enable the safe continuation of the church's ministry.

The Congregational Meeting

A congregational meeting can prove to be a powerful aspect of the ministry of truth telling. However, if thoughtful and prayerful preparation for such a meeting is not done, it can become an occasion of anger and confusion. Therefore, schedule a meeting for a specific time and place and make plans for it. Do not simply say at the time of announcements in the Sunday morning worship service, "As you may have heard, there has been an allegation of child abuse in our church, and now is just as good a time as any to discuss what happened." An impromptu invitation can be far more harmful than helpful. It may force members to participate in a discussion that they would very much prefer to avoid. It may shock members who have heard no previous reports or rumors. It may cause some members to suddenly remember previous trauma in their lives and evoke severe emotional reactions. Such an approach may also insult the family of the child victim by making it appear that child abuse in your church is nothing more than an item on the list of Sunday morning announcements. The consequences of such a cavalier approach, in subsequent litigation, could be harmful for the church.

Plan carefully for a congregational meeting. Give everyone advance notice so they may choose whether to attend. Select the leaders for the meeting very carefully. In most cases, it will be important for the pastor to be a leader. However, if the pastor is the accused abuser, he or she cannot lead the meeting. Also, in most cases, it is important to have lay leaders present as well as representatives from the annual conference (such as the district superintendent). The lay leader will be able to provide information about the actions taken by the church thus far. The district superintendent may not need to do anything more than reinforce the support of the annual conference as the congregation deals with this crisis. Even so, this is a valuable contribution and should not be overlooked. Finally, I believe the leadership team for the congregational meeting should include a qualified counselor who is not necessarily a member of the congregation. Inevitably, this meeting will elicit strong feelings and emotions. By having a counselor present, it is possible to help immediately those who experience strong feelings, instead of putting them off or minimizing the feelings.

Meeting Agenda

What should happen in a congregational meeting following an incident of child abuse? Include the following elements:
- fact sharing
- small group sharing time
- closing moments of reflection and worship

Notes:

MINISTRY AFTER ABUSE must be aimed at assuring justice for all and healing for those who are suffering.

Notes:

IT IS FAR BETTER TO ADMIT not knowing the answer than to speculate about the incident or the outcome.

Open the fact sharing by giving an accurate description of what has happened and what actions have been taken, or will be taken. Answer questions as accurately as possible without jeopardizing any ongoing investigation by the church or local law enforcement agencies. Protect the identity of the victim(s), especially if the family has requested as much privacy as possible. Do not be afraid to answer questions with, "We don't know the answer to that yet." It is far better to admit not knowing the answer than to speculate about the incident or the outcome.

The small group sharing time probably will be the most important segment of this meeting. Divide the total group into small groups of five or six. Have prepared facilitators for each group. Your annual conference may be able to suggest facilitators in your area. The facilitator will begin by letting everyone know that it is permissible to express *any* feeling or emotion within the small group. All will be allowed time to share, and there will be no debate about the feelings or emotions expressed. The purpose of this segment of the meeting is to help people identify and verbalize their feelings about the incident. The purpose is not to strategize a response or elicit premature forgiveness toward the abuser. Be prepared for this part of the meeting to take an hour or more.

When it is apparent that the small groups are able to bring their time together to a close, reassemble the whole group. Acknowledge the reality of this painful situation and offer a prayer for the congregation as it seeks to achieve justice for all involved and healing for all who are suffering.

Continuing Ministry

The initial actions of the church are really only the first steps in what may be a long process of restoring the victim(s) and the congregation to spiritual health. One letter or one congregational meeting probably will not be all your church needs. Based on the feelings, fears, and needs expressed in the congregational meeting, you can develop a plan for continuing ministry. It may be useful to appoint a task force for this planning process, just as you utilized a task force to develop the child abuse prevention policy and procedures. Another approach is to use existing groups within the church to plan appropriate ministries of healing, justice, education, and worship.

As the group begins its work, it will be well advised to consider several types of ministry: educational, supportive, and any others that have been suggested by members of the group.

Educational ministries may include programs on
- the consequences of child abuse.
- how to comfort families suffering from abuse.
- how children and youth can protect themselves from abuse.
- resources in your community for victims/survivors.
- other topics of concern.

Programs may include speakers who are adult survivors of child abuse, and they can tell how they achieved healing and recovery. Programs like these can be carried out through Sunday school classes, youth groups, or other settings. It is important to remember that none of these programs should be provided without advance notice and publicity. In this way you ensure that those who wish to participate can make their plans and that those who do not wish to participate can avoid any involvement.

Support ministries can be developed within your congregation for families suffering as a result of child abuse, as well as for victims of child abuse. Identify qualified leaders within your congregation or community, and enlist their aid in organizing support groups. Providing individual counseling for the victim(s), the families, and other affected members of the congregation can also be a very important ministry. You may be able to make the necessary financial arrangements with a trained and experienced counselor so that the victim(s) and/or families can receive sufficient counseling to achieve healing. This type of ministry may also be very important to the family members of the accused abuser. While it would be inappropriate to condone in any way the behavior of the abuser, it is appropriate to recognize that in this situation the extended family members of the abuser may suffer terribly. Thus, offering counseling to them may be an act of grace and healing without condoning the abusive behavior.

Programming with children and youth aimed at restoring their trust in the church and in its workers will be a valuable support ministry. Programs and discussion groups that focus on justice, mercy, and reconciliation in difficult situations will set a solid foundation for their continuing spiri-

THE MORE A CONGREGATION does to encourage openness and honesty in communication, the faster healing and recovery can proceed.

Notes:

tual growth. Programming of this nature will require extensive planning as well as qualified leadership. No matter how much work is required, it is worth it if one child or youth is enabled to feel safe in the church again.

All of these suggestions for continuing ministries are based on the premise that the more your congregation does to encourage openness and honesty in communication, the faster healing and recovery can proceed. No matter how long the process takes, there are two things that should never be allowed: blaming the victim and offering forgiveness to the abuser without any sign of repentance from the abuser. The child abuse victim is never responsible for being abused and did not do anything to cause it. Therefore, do not let your church attempt to assuage its conscience with words like, "Well, we did all we could to prevent something like this, but she asked for it!" This kind of remark does not foster open and honest communication. Rather, it denies the truth and insults the victim and the victim's family.

There is no benefit to offering premature forgiveness to the abuser. For healing to occur, it is necessary that painful consequences be endured, not just by the victim(s) who suffers first but also by the abuser. Only when the abuser is truly able to live a changed life and demonstrate sorrow and repentance will it be possible for the congregation to offer the grace of forgiveness. Even then, the victim(s) may or may not be able to forgive the harm they have suffered, and no pressure to forgive should ever be brought to bear on the victim(s) simply to help the abuser feel better.

Finally, after enough time has passed, the planning group may want to organize a time for sharing that is similar to that in the first congregational meeting. Use this to assess how much healing and recovery has occurred. Identify any remaining needs or issues that have not been resolved and possible ways to address them. There is a natural tendency to tuck the pain tightly away, creating the need for regular follow-up. In conclusion, provide a worship celebration to express gratitude for the progress that has been made toward healing and recovery, and to express joy in the congregation's united efforts to do justice and to trust in the abiding grace and love of Jesus Christ, our Savior.

Sample Forms

PLEASE NOTE THAT all of the forms, checklists, and other items in this section are samples and need to be modified to meet your specific needs. Permission is given to reproduce these forms for churches who have purchased *Safe Sanctuaries*.

Items include

1. Membership Form for the Local Church Task Force for the Prevention of Child Abuse in the Church

2. Child Abuse Prevention Policy

3. Employment Application

4. Authorization and Request for Criminal Records Check

5. Volunteer Application

6. Form for Reference Check

7. Participation Covenant Statement

8. Report of Suspected Incident of Child Abuse

9. Accident Report Form

10. Local Church Self-Evaluation Form

11. Childcare Worker Position Description

12. Order of Worship: A Celebration of Our Commitment to Children and Youth

MEMBERSHIP FORM FOR THE LOCAL CHURCH TASK FORCE FOR THE PREVENTION OF CHILD ABUSE IN THE CHURCH

Pastor
Name: _____
Address: _____
Phone: _____

Member of Staff-Parish Committee
Name: _____
Address: _____
Phone: _____

Member of Board of Trustees
Name: _____
Address: _____
Phone: _____

Lay Leader
Name: _____
Address: _____
Phone: _____

Minister of Youth/Director of Youth Ministries
Name: _____
Address: _____
Phone: _____

Minister of Children/Director of Children's Ministries
Name: _____
Address: _____
Phone: _____

Director of Any Weekday Program for Children
Name: _____
Address: _____
Phone: _____

Representative from Each Group Working with Children or Youth
(The number of members listed here will depend on the number of groups active in your congregation.)
Name: _____
Address: _____
Phone: _____

Name: _____
Address: _____
Phone: _____

Name: _____
Address: _____
Phone: _____

CHILD ABUSE PREVENTION POLICY

Introduction

The General Conference of The United Methodist Church, in April 1996, adopted a resolution aimed at reducing the risk of child sexual abuse in the church. The adopted resolution includes the following statement:

> Jesus said, Whoever welcomes [a] child...welcomes me." (Matthew 18:5). Children are our present and our future, our hope, our teachers, our inspiration. They are full participants in the life of the church and in the realm of God.
>
> Jesus also said, "If any of you put a stumbling block before one of these little ones..., it would be better for you if a great millstone were fastened around your neck and you were drowned in the depth of the sea." (Matthew 18:6). Our Christian faith calls us to offer both hospitality and protection to the little ones, the children. The Social Principles of The United Methodist Church state that "...children must be protected from economic, physical and sexual exploitation, and abuse."
>
> Tragically, churches have not always been safe places for children. Child sexual abuse, exploitation and ritual abuse (ritual abuse refers to abusive acts committed as part of ceremonies or rites; ritual abusers are often related to cults, or pretend to be) occur in churches, both large and small, urban and rural. The problem cuts across all economic, cultural and racial lines. It is real, and it appears to be increasing. Most annual conferences can cite specific incidents of child sexual abuse and exploitation in their churches. Virtually every congregation has among its members adult survivors of early sexual trauma.
>
> Such incidents are devastating to all who are involved: the child, the family, the local church and its leaders. Increasingly, churches are torn apart by the legal, emotional, and monetary consequences of litigation following allegations of abuse.
>
> God calls us to make our churches safe places, protecting children and other vulnerable persons from sexual and ritual abuse. God calls us to create communities of faith where children and adults grow safe and strong. (From *The Book of Resolutions of The United Methodist Church—1996*. Copyright © 1996 by The United Methodist Publishing House. Used by permission. [pp. 384-386])

Thus, in covenant with all United Methodist congregations, we adopt this policy for the prevention of child abuse in our church.

Purpose

Our congregation's purpose for establishing this Child Abuse Prevention Policy and accompanying procedures is to demonstrate our absolute and unwavering commitment to the physical safety and spiritual growth of all of our children and youth.

Statement of Covenant

Therefore, as a Christian community of faith and a United Methodist congregation, we pledge to conduct the ministry of the gospel in ways that assure the safety and spiritual growth of all of our children and youth as well as all of the workers with children and youth. We will follow reasonable safety measures in the selection and recruitment of workers; we will implement prudent operational procedures in all programs and events; we will educate all of our workers with children and youth regarding the use of all appropriate policies and methods (including first aid and methods of discipline); we will have a clearly defined procedure for reporting a suspected incident of abuse that conforms to the requirements of state law; and we will be prepared to respond to media inquiries if an incident occurs.

Conclusion

In all of our ministries with children and youth, this congregation is committed to demonstrating the love of Jesus Christ so that each child will be "...surrounded by steadfast love, ...established in the faith, and confirmed and strengthened in the way that leads to life eternal" ("Baptismal Covenant II," *United Methodist Hymnal*, p. 44).

EMPLOYMENT APPLICATION

(This type of application should be completed by all who seek any position that will involve the supervision and/or custody of children or youth. You should tailor the application to the specific circumstances in your congregation. However, the employment application should include, at a minimum, sections for personal identification, job qualifications, experience and background, references, and a waiver/consent to a criminal records check.)

Name: _____
Last   First   Middle

Are you over the age of 18?   ☐ Yes   ☐ No

Present address:_____

City: _____ State: _____ Zip:_____

Home phone: _____

Position applied for: _____

Date you are available to start: _____

Qualifications:

Academic achievements: (Schools attended, degrees earned, dates of completion)

_____

_____

_____

Continuing education completed: (Courses taken, dates of completion)

_____

_____

_____

Professional organizations: (List any in which you have membership)

_____

_____

_____

First aid training?   ☐ Yes   ☐ No   Date completed_____

CPR training?   ☐ Yes   ☐ No   Date completed _____

Previous Work Experience: Please list your previous employers from the past five years. Include the job title, a description of position duties and responsibilities, the name of the company/employer, the address of company/employer, the name of your immediate supervisor, and the dates you were employed in each position.

_____

_____

_____

_____

_____

_____

Previous Volunteer Experience: Please list any relevant volunteer positions you have held and list the duties you performed in each position, the name of your supervisor, the address and phone number of the volunteer organization, and the dates of your volunteer service.

_____

_____

_____

_____

_____

_____

Have you ever been convicted of or pled guilty to a crime, either a midemeanor or a felony (including but not limited to drug-related charges, child abuse, other crimes of violence, theft, or motor vehicle violations)? ☐ No   ☐ Yes

If yes, please explain:

_____

_____

Employment Application, p. 2

References: Please list three individuals who are not related to you by blood or marriage as references. Please list people who have known you for at least three years.

1. Name: _____
   Address: _____
   Daytime Phone: _____
   Evening Phone: _____
   Length of time you have known reference: _____
   Relationship to reference: _____

2. Name: _____
   Address: _____
   Daytime Phone: _____
   Evening Phone: _____
   Length of time you have known reference: _____
   Relationship to reference: _____

3. Name: _____
   Address: _____
   Daytime Phone: _____
   Evening Phone: _____
   Length of time you have known reference: _____
   Relationship to reference: _____

Waiver and Consent:

I, _____, hereby certify that the information I have provided on this application for employment is true and correct. I authorize this church to verify the information I have provided on this application by contacting the references and employers I have listed, by conducting a criminal records check, or by other means, including contacting others whom I have not listed. I authorize the references and employers listed in this application to give you whatever information they may have regarding my character and fitness for the job for which I have applied. Furthermore, I waive any rights I may have to confidentiality.

In the event that my application is accepted and I become employed by _____ Church, I agree to abide by and be bound by the policies of _____ Church and to refrain from inappropriate conduct in the performance of my duties on behalf of _____ Church.

I have read this waiver and the entire application, and I am fully aware of its contents. I sign this consent freely and under no duress or coercion.

_____   _____
Signature of Applicant   Date

_____   _____
Witness   Date

This is a sample form. Please tailor your congregation's form to comply with the reporting requirements of the laws of your state and your congregation's policies.
Sample Employment Application, p. 3

AUTHORIZATION AND REQUEST FOR CRIMINAL RECORDS CHECK

I, _____ , hereby authorize _____ Church to request the _____ police/sheriff's department to release information regarding any record of charges or convictions contained in its files, or in any criminal file maintained on me, whether said file is a local, state, or national file, and including but not limited to accusations and convictions for crimes committed against minors, to the fullest extent permitted by state and federal law. I do release said police/sheriff's department from all liability that may result from any such disclosure made in response to this request.

_____

Signature of Applicant   Date

Print applicant's full name:_____

Print all other names that have been used by applicant (if any):

_____

Date of birth:_____ Place of birth:_____

Social Security number (if required by sheriff's dept.)_____

Driver's license number: _____ State issuing license:_____

License expiration date: _____

Request sent to:_____

Name: _____

Address: _____

Phone:_____

This is a sample form. Your local police department or sheriff's department may have its own request form and prefer that you use it.

VOLUNTEER APPLICATION

Name: _____

Address: _____

Daytime phone: _____ Evening phone: _____

Occupation: _____

Employer: _____

Current job responsibilities and schedule: _____

_____

Previous work experience: _____

Previous volunteer experience: _____

_____

Special interests, hobbies, and skills: _____

How many hours per week are you available to volunteer? _____

_____ Days _____ Evenings _____ Weekends

Can you make a one-year commitment to this volunteer role? _____

Do you have your own transportation? _____

Do you have a valid driver's license? _____

Do you have liability insurance? (list policy limits and name of carrier) _____

Why would you like to volunteer as a worker with children and/or youth?

_____

_____

What qualities do you have that would help you work with children and/or youth?

_____

_____

How were you parented as a child? _____

_____

How do you discipline your own children? _____

Have you ever been charged, convicted of, or pled guilty to a crime, either a midemeanor or a felony (including but not limited to drug-related charges, child abuse, other crimes of violence, theft, or motor vehicle violations)?   ☐ No   ☐ Yes

If yes, please explain fully:

_____

_____

Have you ever been exposed to an incident of child abuse or neglect?   ☐ No   ☐ Yes

If yes, how did you feel about the incident?_____

Would you be available for periodic volunteer training sessions?   ☐ Yes   ☐ No

References: Please list three personal references (people who are not related to you by blood or marriage) and provide a complete address and phone information for each. References are confidential.

1. Name: _____

   Address: _____

   Daytime phone: _____

   Evening phone:_____

   Relationship to reference: _____

2. Name: _____

   Address: _____

   Daytime phone: _____

   Evening phone:_____

   Relationship to reference: _____

3. Name: _____

   Address: _____

   Daytime phone: _____

   Evening phone:_____

   Relationship to reference: _____

_____
Signature of Applicant   Date

This is a sample form. Use it as a guide for tailoring your own application based on your congregation's needs.

Sample Volunteer Application, p. 2

FORM FOR REFERENCE CHECK

Applicant name: _____

Reference name: _____

Reference address: _____

Reference phone: _____

1. What is your relationship to the applicant?

2. How long have you known the applicant?

3. How well do you know the applicant?

4. How would you describe the applicant?

5. How would you describe the applicant's ability to relate to children and/or youth?

6. How would you describe the applicant's ability to relate to adults?

7. How would you describe the applicant's leadership abilities?

8. How would you feel about having the applicant as a volunteer worker with your child and/or youth?

9. Do you know of any characteristics that would negatively affect the applicant's ability to work with children and/or youth? If so, please describe.

10. Do you have any knowledge that the applicant has ever been convicted of a crime? If so, please describe.

11. Please list any other comments you would like to make:

Reference inquiry completed by: _____
                                   Signature   Date

This is a sample form. Please tailor it to the specific needs of your local congregation.

PARTICIPATION COVENANT STATEMENT

The congregation of _____ Church is committed to providing a safe and secure environment for all children, youth, and volunteers who participate in ministries and activities sponsored by the church. The following policy statements reflect our congregation's commitment to preserving this church as a holy place of safety and protection for all who would enter and as a place in which all people can experience the love of God through relationships with others.

1. No adult who has been convicted of child abuse (either sexual abuse, physical abuse, or emotional abuse) should volunteer to work with children or youth in any church-sponsored activity.
2. Adult survivors of child abuse need the love and support of our congregation. Any adult survivor who desires to volunteer in some capacity to work with children or youth is encouraged to discuss his/her willingness with one of our church's ministers before accepting an assignment.
3. All adult volunteers involved with children or youth of our church must have been members of the congregation for at least six months before beginning a volunteer assignment.
4. Adult volunteers with children and youth shall observe the "Two-Adult Rule" at all times so that no adult is ever alone with children or youth.
5. Adult volunteers with children and youth shall attend regular training and educational events provided by the church to keep volunteers informed of church policies and state laws regarding child abuse.
6. Adult volunteers shall immediately report to their supervisor any behavior that seems abusive or inappropriate.

Please answer each of the following questions:

1. As a volunteer in this congregation, do you agree to observe and abide by all church policies regarding working in ministries with children and youth? ☐ Yes ☐ No
2. As a volunteer in this congregation, do you agree to observe the "Two-Adult Rule" at all times? ☐ Yes ☐ No
3. As a volunteer in this congregation, do you agree to abide by the six-month rule before beginning a volunteer assignment? ☐ Yes ☐ No
4. As a volunteer in this congregation, do you agree to participate in training and education events provided by the church related to your volunteer assignment? ☐ Yes ☐ No
5. As a volunteer in this congregation, do you agree to promptly report abusive or inappropriate behavior to your supervisor? ☐ Yes ☐ No
6. As a volunteer in this congregation, do you agree to discuss with a minister of this congregation your experience, if any, as a survivor of child abuse? ☐ Yes ☐ No
   (Answering yes to this question does not automatically disqualify you from volunteering with children or youth.)
7. As a volunteer in this congregation, do you agree to inform a minister of this congregation if you have ever been convicted of child abuse? ☐ Yes ☐ No

I have read this **Participation Covenant**, and I agree to observe and abide by the policies set forth above.

_____
Signature of Applicant   Date

_____
Print full name

This is a sample form. Please tailor it to fit your congregation's specific needs.

REPORT OF SUSPECTED INCIDENT OF CHILD ABUSE

1. Name of worker (paid or volunteer) observing or receiving disclosure of child abuse: _____

    _____

2. Victim's name: _____

    Victim's age/date of birth: _____

3. Date/place of initial conversation with/report from victim: _____

    _____

4. Victim's statement (give your detailed summary here):_____

    _____

    _____

    _____

    _____

5. Name of person accused of abuse: _____

    Relationship of accused to victim (paid staff, volunteer, family member, other): _____

    _____

6. Reported to pastor:_____

    Date/time: _____

    Summary: _____

    _____

    _____

    _____

7. Call to victim's parent/guardian: _____

    Date/time: _____

    Spoke with: _____

    Summary: _____

    _____

    _____

8. Call to local children and family service agency: _____

    Date/time: _____

    Spoke with: _____

    Summary: _____

    _____

    _____

9. Call to local law enforcement agency: _____

    Date/time: _____

    Spoke with: _____

    Summary: _____

    _____

    _____

10. Other contacts: _____

    Name: _____

    Date/time: _____

    Summary: _____

    _____

    _____

_____

Signature of Applicant   Date

This is a sample form. Please tailor your congregation's form to comply with the reporting requirements of the laws of your state and your congregation's policies.

Note: It is imperative that the person filling out this report be familiar with the state law reporting requirements before taking any action or completing this report.

Report of Suspected Incident of Child Abuse, p. 2

ACCIDENT REPORT FORM

(Please print all information.)

Date of accident: _____ Time of accident: _____

Name of child/youth injured:_____ Age: _____

Address of child/youth: _____

_____

Location of accident: _____

Parent or guardian: _____

Name of person(s) who witnessed the accident:_____

   Name: _____ Phone: _____

   Name: _____ Phone: _____

   Name: _____ Phone: _____

Describe accident:

_____

_____

_____

_____

*This is a sample form. Please tailor it to fit your congregation's specific needs.

LOCAL CHURCH SELF-EVALUATION FORM

Use the following list to help your congregation assess its policy needs for the prevention of child abuse in your church. Read each statement, and mark the appropriate response in the column to the right. By completing the form, you will be able to see at a glance the areas needing attention.

Statement	Yes	No	Unsure
1. We screen and check references for all paid employees, including clergy, who have significant contact with children or youth.	☐	☐	☐
2. We screen all volunteer workers for any position involving work with children or youth.	☐	☐	☐
3. We train at least annually all volunteer or paid workers with children or youth to understand the nature of child abuse.	☐	☐	☐
4. We train at least annually all volunteer or paid workers with children or youth in how to carry out our policies to prevent child abuse.	☐	☐	☐
5. Our workers are informed of state law requirements regarding child abuse and their responsibility for reporting incidents.	☐	☐	☐
6. We have a clear reporting procedure for a suspected incident of child abuse that follows the requirements of our state law.	☐	☐	☐
7. We have insurance coverage available in case a child abuse complaint occurs.	☐	☐	☐
8. We have a clearly defined building usage strategy as a component of our child abuse prevention plan.	☐	☐	☐
9. We have a clearly defined response plan to be implemented in case an allegation of child abuse is made against someone in our church.	☐	☐	☐
10. We offer at least annual educational opportunities to parents of children and youth about how to recognize and how to reduce risks of child abuse.	☐	☐	☐
11. We take our policies to prevent child abuse seriously, and we are committed to their enforcement for the safety and security of all of our children.	☐	☐	☐

CHILDCARE WORKER POSITION DESCRIPTION

Position: Childcare worker in the church nurseries
Reports to: Nursery Supervisor/Coordinator

General qualifications required

1. All childcare staff members shall be of good character and be of the Christian faith.
2. All childcare staff members shall
   a. be physically, mentally, and emotionally healthy.
   b. have a basic understanding of children and their needs.
   c. be adaptive to a variety of situations.
   d. be willing to grow in their knowledge of children through periodic education and training events.
3. All childcare staff members shall have a physician's report stating that the staff member is in good health and has presented the result of a current Tuberculin test.
4. _____ Church hires without regard to race, sex, or national origin.

Educational qualifications required

All childcare staff members shall have completed the equivalent of a high school diploma.

Duties of childcare staff member

1. Provide physical, emotional, and intellectual support and stimulation to each child in your care, as appropriate for the circumstances.
2. Provide appropriate guidance to each child in your care.
3. Develop a relationship of trust and continuity with the children in your care, which will enhance each child's development of positive self images.
4. Provide support and assistance to parents when they arrive with their child.

Performance expectations of a childcare staff member

1. Be punctual. Notify the nursery supervisor in advance if you must be late.
2. Be reliable in your attendance. Notify the nursery supervisor in advance if you must be absent.
3. Attend periodic training and education events provided by the church.
4. Be polite, friendly, and courteous to others, both children and adults.
5. Do not engage in physical punishment/discipline of any child.
6. Cooperate with other childcare staff and with parents.
7. Abide by and apply the childcare policies of _____ Church at all times.

I have read the position description for childcare staff members of _____
Church and understand its contents. My signature below indicates my agreement and covenant to abide by the requirements set forth above.

_____
Signature of Applicant   Date

This is a sample form. Please adapt it to the specific needs of your congregation.

A Celebration of Our Commitment to Children and Youth

Prelude
"A Mighty Fortress Is Our God" (*United Methodist Hymnal*, No. 110)

Call to Worship
Leader: O God, by our presence here today,
People: *We welcome the children!*
Leader: O God, by our promise in Holy Baptism,
People: *We welcome the children!*
Leader: O God, by our participation in the ministries of this congregation,
People: *We welcome the children!*
Leader: O God, by our commitment to keeping this place holy and safe in every way,
People: *We welcome the children!*
Leader: O God, in this time of worship, fill our hearts with joy as
People: *We welcome the children!*
Leader: O God, give us wisdom, strength, and courage enough to show the world that
ALL: *We welcome the children! AMEN!*

Hymn of Praise
"This Is the Day!" (*United Methodist Hymnal*, No. 657)
(Lead the congregation in singing this hymn as a round: first group–the children's choir; second group–all male voices; third group–all female voices.)

Congregational Prayer
Gracious and most merciful God, you have brought us together in witness to your love of all children and youth. Open our hearts and minds in this moment and prepare us to receive your message. Show us your will and fill us to overflowing with courage enough to preserve our church as a safe and holy place where our children and youth may grow in faith and in their knowledge of your presence in their lives! Amen.

Pastoral Concerns
Silent Prayer
Pastoral Prayer
The Lord's Prayer

Old Testament Lesson
Micah 6:6-8 (Have a junior-high female read this passage. Or both a junior-high female and male could read it together, in unison, as a powerful and different way to proclaim the Word.)

Congregational Singing or Children's Choir
"I'm Goin'a Sing When the Spirit Says Sing" (*United Methodist Hymnal*, No. 333)
"We Are the Church" (*United Methodist Hymnal*, No. 558)

Gospel Lesson
Matthew 19:13-15 (Have the Gospel read by a senior-high male. Suggest that the reader dress in a costume as Jesus.)

Response to the Gospel
"Heleluyan" (*United Methodist Hymnal*, No. 78)

Epistle Lesson
1 Corinthians 13:1-13 (Have a nursery worker or a grandparent from your congregation read this lesson.)

Affirmation of Faith
(*United Methodist Hymnal*, Nos. 883 or 887)

Recognition of Task Force Members
Invite all members of the task force that developed the child abuse prevention policy to come forward in the sanctuary. Describe the work they have done, and express gratitude and appreciation for their service. Present a guardian angel lapel pin or other appropriate item as a token of appreciation for their work on behalf of children and youth.

Recognition of All Workers with Children and Youth
Invite all members who work with children and youth to stand. Express gratitude and appreciation for their time and devotion to our children and youth. Lead in a round of applause.

Passing of the Peace

Offertory Anthem (by the congregation or youth choir)
"Morning Has Broken" (*United Methodist Hymnal*, No. 145)
"God of the Sparrow
        God of the Whale" (*United Methodist Hymnal*, No. 122)

Doxology
(*United Methodist Hymnal*, No. 95)

Sermon
"We Are Our Children's Safe Sanctuary" (based on the Gospel and Epistle lessons)

Invitation to Christian Discipleship

Hymn of Dedication
"Jesus' Hands Were Kind Hands" (*United Methodist Hymnal*, No. 273)

Benediction

Response Hymn
"Pass It On" (*United Methodist Hymnal*, No. 572)

Other Sources and Resources

These organizations have helpful information and resource materials about child abuse. Materials from these organizations are available upon request.

Organizations:

Childhelp USA
6463 Independence Avenue
Woodland Hills, CA 91367

**National Center for
Missing and Exploited Children**
2101 Wilson Boulevard, Suite 550
Arlington, VA 22201

**National Committee to
Prevent Child Abuse (NCPCA)**
332 South Michigan Avenue, Suite 1600
Chicago, IL 60604

**Center for the Prevention of
Sexual and Domestic Violence**
936 North 34th Street, Suite 200
Seattle, WA 98103

**General Commission on the
Status and Role of Women**
1200 Davis Street
Evanston, IL 60201
847/869-7330

Nonprofit Risk Management Center
1001 Connecticut Avenue, NW, Suite 900
Washington, DC 20036

United Methodist Communications
810 12th Avenue South
Nashville, TN 37203
615/742-5400

Children's Defense Fund
25 E Street NW
Washington, DC 20001

**Your state and/or county child and
family protective services department.**

Risk Management Department
General Council on Finance and Admin.
1200 Davis Street
Evanston, IL 60201-4193
847/869-3345

**The National Court-Appointed
Special Advocate Association**
100 West Harrison Street
North Tower, Suite 500
Seattle, WA 98119-4123

**National Clearinghouse on
Child Abuse and Neglect Information**
PO Box 1182
Washington, DC 20013-1182

**National Center for
Prosecution of Child Abuse**
99 Canal Center Plaza
Alexandria, VA 22314

National Children's Advocacy Center
200 Westside Square
Huntsville, AL 35801

Parents' Anonymous
520 South Lafayette Park Place, Suite 316
Los Angeles, CA 90045

Christian Ministry Resources
PO Box 1098
Matthews, NC 28106

Office of Childrens Ministries
General Board of Discipleship
PO Box 840
Nashville, TN 37202-0840
615/340-7143

Sources:

These resources will guide you to many other helpful resources related to child abuse.

Besharov, Douglas J. *Recognizing Child Abuse: A Guide for the Concerned.* New York: The Free Press, 1990.

Carlson, Lee W. *Child Sexual Abuse: A Handbook for Clergy and Church Members.* Valley Forge, PA: Judson Press, 1988.

Children's Defense Fund. *Welcome the Child: A Child Advocacy Guide for Churches.* Washington, DC: Children's Defense Fund, 1994.

Criminal History Record Checks: A Report for Nonprofits. The National Assembly of National Voluntary Health and Social Welfare Organizations, Washington, DC: 1991.

Fortune, Rev. Marie M. *Love Does No Harm: Sexual Ethics for the Rest of Us.* New York: The Continuum Publishing Group, 1995. (Available from the Center for the Prevention of Sexual and Domestic Violence.)

Fortune, Rev. Marie M. *Violence in the Family: A Workshop Curriculum for Clergy and Other Helpers.* Cleveland: The Pilgrim Press, 1991. (Available from the Center for the Prevention of Sexual and Domestic Violence.)

Heggen, Carolyn H. *Sexual Abuse in Christian Homes and Churches.* Scottdale, PA: Herald Press, 1993.

Horton, Anne L. and Judith A. Williamson (eds.). *Abuse & Religion: When Praying Isn't Enough.* Lexington, MA: Lexington Books, 1988.

Lew, Mike. *Victims No Longer: Men Recovering from Incest and Other Childhood Sexual Abuse.* New York: HarperCollins Publishers, Inc., 1990.

Olsen, Harriet J. (ed.). *The Book of Discipline of The United Methodist Church—1996.* Nashville: The United Methodist Publishing House, 1996.

Patterson, John with Charles Tremper and Pam Rypkema. *Staff Screening Tool Kit: Keeping the Bad Apples Out of Your Organization.* Washington, DC: Nonprofit Risk Management Center, 1994.

Public Media Division of United Methodist Communications. *Not If, But When.* Nashville: 1993.

Reid, Rev. Kathryn Goering. *Preventing Child Sexual Abuse: A Curriculum for Children Ages 5-8.* Cleveland: United Church Press, 1994. (Available from the Center for the Prevention of Sexual and Domestic Violence.)

_____, with Rev. Marie M. Fortune. *Preventing Child Sexual Abuse: A Curriculum for Children Ages 9-12.* New York: The Pilgrim Press, 1990. (Available from the Center for the Prevention of Sexual and Domestic Violence.)

Rose, Emilie P. (pseud.) *Reaching for the Light: A Guide for Ritual Abuse Survivors and Their Therapists.* Cleveland: The Pilgrim Press, 1996.

Voelkel-Haugen, Rebecca and Rev. Marie M. Fortune. *Sexual Abuse Prevention: A Course of Study for Teenagers.* Louisville: Westminister John Knox Press, 1996. (Available from the Center for the Prevention of Sexual and Domestic Violence.)

Videos:

Caring Shepherds. (18 minutes) Produced by and available from the Risk Management Department of the General Council on Finance and Administration of The United Methodist Church. Created to help congregational leaders identify potential problems and develop policies to reduce the occurence of sexual abuse and misconduct.

Ask Before You Hug: Sexual Harassment in the Church. (31 minutes) Produced by United Methodist Communications. Available from EcuFilm (800/251-4091). Helps clarify what constitutes sexual harassment.

Hear Their Cries. (48-minutes) Available from the Center for the Prevention of Sexual and Domestic Violence. Provides definitions, signs for recognizing abuse, and examples of how to respond.

Bless Our Children: Preventing Sexual Abuse. (40 minutes) Available from the Center for the Prevention of Sexual and Domestic Violence. Story of one congregation's efforts to provide abuse prevention information for their children.